Entertaining with Love

Entertaining with Love

INSPIRED RECIPES FOR EVERYDAY ENTERTAINING

WRITTEN BY

Marc J. Sievers

DESIGN & PHOTOGRAPHY BY

Ryan L. Sievers

MARC-RYAN GROUP

CHICAGO

ЯM

Published in the United States by Marc-Ryan Group

Marc-Ryan Group
Chicago Illinois USA
Visit our web site at www.marc-ryan.com

First Edition: September 2012

Sievers, Marc J.
Entertaining with Love: Inspired recipes for everyday
entertaining / Marc J. Sievers and Ryan L. Sievers – 1st ed.
Includes recipe index.

ISBN 978-0-615-69069-8

Printed in the United States of America | 5

The name Marc-Ryan Group, the stylized 'RM' symbol, and the 'RM' circle
symbols are trademarks or registered trademarks of Marc-Ryan Group,
Chicago USA.

At the time of publication, the name Veuve and signature yellow trade dress is
a trademark or registered trademark of Veuve Clicquot Ponsardin, a division
of LVMH Moët Hennessy - Louis Vuitton, Paris France. The name Morton
Salt and the girl with umbrella motif are trademarks or registered trademarks
of Morton Salt, Inc., a division of K+S Aktiengesellschaft, Kassel, Germany.

*I dedicate this book to all of my family and friends,
old and new, who have helped to sustain in me a love
for food and the gatherings that always end up in
the kitchen.*

WITH MY LOVE,

Marc
xo

ЯМ

I offer my gratitude to

RITA MADONNA BERUBE
'NAN'
For your lessons of love in the kitchen and beyond

AUNTIE DENISE & UNCLE DAN
For being my most inspiring role-models for a life best lived

AHREN & BROOKE
For your unconditional support and love

RYAN'S MOM & DAD
For making the kitchen a part of Ryan's life from the beginning

JANET & TONY
For being my most willing and supportive taste-testers

WITH MY MOST HEART-FELT THANK YOU,

MARC

Introduction

LESSONS OF LOVE—INSPIRATION FROM MY KITCHEN TO YOURS

Being in the kitchen, cooking, and entertaining have been my passion for as long as I can remember. It was about time that I put my experience and expertise into a format that I could share with you, which would inspire you to try a new recipe or plan and host a great party. It is in the kitchen, around the table, for Friday evening cocktails, holidays, and so many other everyday events in our lives that we entertain with love. May these recipes for everyday entertaining be an inspiration from my kitchen to yours!

For the longest time I can remember I have been enamored with being in the kitchen and entertaining. Like so many of us, my family is my extended family. It is big and close-knit. My Nan was, for most of her life, the matriarch of our noisy and affable troupe. She watched over us, pushed us, and most of all loved us. Her greatest gift to me was sharing her experience and wisdom with me, ever so patiently and thoughtfully. From a grandmother to a grandson, that involved a lot of territory and subject matter. But in the context of this, my first cook book, one of her many great lessons—taught to me collectively over the course of my formative years—was to show me just how magical of a place the kitchen could be.

No matter the path I have taken or the turn of events in my life, the kitchen has always been the place where I feel the most comfortable. In the kitchen I can create a soothing and warm feel-good meal to help brush off a bad day. I can put on my thinking cap to experiment with, and explore, new ideas. The kitchen is a place for me to get lost in a fairytale of cakes and frosting, or don my apron and whip up amazing first, second, and third courses. For me, the kitchen is where I can push my own boundaries and feel confident doing it.

Certainly it wasn't always like that, but I have had some good lessons along the way. From my Nan sparking that first bit of curiosity in my heart, to the indomitable Julia Child encouraging me (along with generations before and after) to be brave and dare to try, I have spent my life absorbing, learning, and practicing. And it is in the practice of the art of cooking that I have found a true passion.

Though I have not spent my career in a professional kitchen, I have spent the majority of my life learning and applying my talent as an elevated home cook and entertaining expert. At every possible opportunity I have practiced until perfected, and that has enabled me to bring together my expertise to share with you.

Throughout my career and personal life I have always had a flair for entertaining and an eye for well-executed style. The fun of being in the kitchen and cooking has been one part of the whole. My mind simply does not stop with just making a recipe into a nicely plated dish. I am also thinking about complimenting my dish with the right table setting, music selection, flowers, and so many other details. I see a symphony—and sometimes a grand opera—of elements that can be coordinated and harmonized to create a fantastic and memorable experience. Altogether I consider this to be the essence of entertaining and creating memorable experiences.

Over the course of my creative career I have honed simple techniques, useful tips, and little tricks to eliminate unnecessary complexity—often a deterrent for people to spend time in the kitchen or entertain. In fact, one of my motivations has been to take the stress and complication out of the equation of entertaining. I think most people feel as I do—we have no desire to feel dead tired and look haggard when trying to entertain. What would be the fun in that? I believe in enjoying the process of making delicious home-cooked dishes,

sharing them with family and friends, and being able to partake in my own festivities!

That sentiment has led me to the creation of this cookbook—to share with you, in a rather more organized fashion, the knowledge I have developed and the expertise I have gained along my own journey. And quite happily, I have not done this alone.

My husband Ryan and I have been a team since we first met. And it has been with his love and support that I have been able to produce this cookbook. I have gained not only from his loving encouragement, but also his business acumen and design talent. This cookbook has come together as a team effort thanks to his inspiration, guidance, and calming reassurance along the way. Together with Ryan I feel and know that we can accomplish any dream that we make our own. This first cookbook is a testament to our determination as a loving team.

Though Ryan and I grew up in different parts of the country and with different experiences, we were actually raised much in the same way. It is in that dual similarity and difference that we have found we complement one another rather than duplicate each other. Perhaps we did not know the full extent of how much that was true when we first met, but it became apparent very quickly—on our first date, in fact!

We both knew the other was The One after just a few months. Our second date had us in the kitchen dying Easter eggs. Our third and fourth dates involved elaborate and delicious home-cooked meals aimed to impress. It worked, for us both! The kitchen has been a recurring backdrop to our relationship from the very beginning.

As Ryan has described my presence in the kitchen, I am "a whirl-wind of off-the-cuff creativity, whipping together fantastically delicious meals, and baking magically decadent desserts that surprise and delight." That of course made me blush until he followed it up with a rather accurate observation that, "in his creative wake he tends to leave an equally impressive pile of dishes and utensils for me, his 'sous chef' husband, to arrange into the dishwasher."

In almost comical contrast, Ryan chops and dices into neatly organized ingredient bowls, clears the decks, and washes as he goes. Methodically organized, from his herbs to his order of operations, Ryan whips up delicious meals that excite my palate every time.

Together, we have fun in the kitchen. We scuffle over who gets to dice the onions or stir the pot, and we constantly bounce ideas off of one another. Our dishes are better, more delicious, and more creative because of one another. And, we love to share our passion for food with our friends and family. In essence, we entertain with love, and from our hearts. Our journey together has been about doing what we love, and loving what we do. Happily for us both that involves a lot of time in the kitchen and at the table together.

Writing this cookbook has been a fantastic exercise of organization for my years of elevated home-cooking and entertaining expertise. In this first edition I share with you easy-to-follow recipes that will help you to excite

and enchant your guests! I have laid out my tried-and-true entertaining techniques that will enable you to quickly plan, prep, and host a fantastic party—while being able to enjoy yourself throughout the process of cooking and entertaining. I have prepared for you here a cooking and entertaining guide that will help you to reach that next level of accomplishment in the kitchen and at the table.

I am often ask, "How do you do it?" by first-time (as well as frequent) guests to my events. This cookbook is my answer. You have already completed my first bit of advice—to find a reliable and easy to read cookbook with recipes and ideas that appeal to you. Next is to get started. It is as simple as picking a recipe and walking through it.

Similarly, entertaining is a very personal affair. From the moment you arrive as a guest to a great soirée you should get an impression of the host's personality and sense of occasion. In these pages you will find the fool-proof techniques, tips, and tricks that I have developed over the years to help you shine through!

Keep this book in the kitchen, and use it thoroughly. I hope the pages will get dog-eared and inked up with your own personal notes. I expect a splatter of sauce will inevitably stain and the cover and the pages to eventually be dusted in flour as you make this cookbook your own!

So, let's get started. May the cooking and entertaining begin!

Fabulous Recipes

DELICIOUS AND EASY RECIPES FOR ANY OCCASION

Great entertaining starts with fabulous food as the first paint to hit your canvas. Cooking for hours and looking ragged by the time your guests arrive is not the start to a fabulous time. Here you will find straight-forward and uncomplicated recipes that can be made without too much fuss, while maintaining a high wow-factor!

May the cooking begin!

Good Morning

GREAT IDEAS FOR A SIMPLE AND CHIC BREAKFAST OR BRUNCH

Eggs Provençal

FOR A SOPHISTICATED AND COMFORTING MORNING MEAL

DIRECTIONS

In a large bowl crack the eggs and whisk vigorously until the whites and yolks are completely incorporated and the mixture is a pale yellow. Set aside.

In a large sauté pan set over medium heat, heat the olive oil. Once hot add onions and season with 1 teaspoon of salt and 2 teaspoons of cracked black pepper. Sauté for 7 to 9 minutes or until translucent and slightly tender. Next, add the garlic and sauté for another 1 to 2 minutes. Reduce the heat to medium-low. Add the butter to the center of the pan and melt.

Next, add the shredded mozzarella to the egg mixture, then add the rosemary, thyme, 1 teaspoon of salt, and 1 teaspoon of cracked black pepper. Whisk vigorously to thoroughly mix and immediately pour into the center of the sauté pan.

Gently stir the eggs, constantly scraping the bottom and sides of the pan with a spatula. The mixture will slowly come together and begin to thicken. Remove from the heat after about 8 minutes, when the eggs are wet-looking and gooey, but no longer runny. Continue to gently stir off the heat for another minute.

Next, transfer the eggs to the center of a serving platter. Top with fresh arugula. Drizzle a bit of olive oil over the leaves, and garnish with big shavings of parmesan cheese.

Serve immediately.

INGREDIENTS

Eggs – 12 extra-large

Yellow Onion – 1 medium, ¼-inch diced

Garlic – 6 cloves, finely minced

Rosemary – 3 tablespoons, fresh, finely minced

Thyme – 3 tablespoons, fresh, finely minced

Mozzarella – 1 cup, shredded

Olive Oil – 3 tablespoons

Kosher Salt – 2 teaspoons, divided

Black Pepper – 3 teaspoons, divided

Arugula – 3 cups, pre-washed

Butter – 2 tablespoons, unsalted

Parmesan Cheese – For garnish

PREPARATION NOTES

Yield – Serves 6

ANOTHER IDEA

You can also plate the eggs for each guest individually for a more formal feel. Divide the eggs between six plates and top each with ½ cup of arugula.

TIP

You cannot rush great eggs! They must cook on a medium-low heat; otherwise they will become tough and dry.

NOTES

_____

_____

_____

_____

_____

_____

_____

_____

French Brioche Rolls

THE MOST AUTHENTIC WAY TO MAKE YOUR HOME SMELL LIKE A PARISIAN PÂTISSERIE

DIRECTIONS

First Day

Begin by sifting the flour and salt into a medium bowl. Set aside.

In a small sauce pan over medium heat, gently heat the milk and butter to just below the simmering point. Add sugar and stir until completely dissolved. Remove from heat and let cool.

In the bowl of an electric mixer fitted with a paddle attachment, combine the hot tap water and yeast and stir with your fingers to fully dissolve. Let stand for 2 to 3 minutes.

Next, with the mixer set to low speed, add the cooled milk mixture and eggs to the water and dissolved yeast. Mix until well incorporated, about 1 to 2 minutes.

Then, with the mixer on medium speed, add 3 cups of flour and mix for 5 minutes. Next, with the mixer still running, add the remaining flour and beat until smooth.

Scrape down the bowl and transfer the dough into a large, well-buttered glass bowl. Cover with a clean dish towel and let rise in a warm place for 1 hour or until the dough doubles in size.

Once the dough has doubled in size, stir the dough. It will deflate a bit. Cover the bowl tightly with plastic wrap and transfer into the refrigerator overnight.

Next Day

Remove the dough from the refrigerator and prepare to hand role two sizes of dough balls. The first should be half the size of the muffin cups in the muffin tin. The smaller dough balls should be half the size of the larger dough balls.

Place the larger dough balls directly into the buttered muffin pans and flatten down slightly. Top each one with a small dough ball.

Brush with a beaten egg and let rise again in a warm spot until they have doubled in size, about 1 hour.

Preheat oven to 400 degrees F.

Bake for 12 to 15 minutes, or until golden brown.

Remove pans from the oven and let cool for 5 minutes before serving. You can also store the brioche rolls in an air tight container once they have cooled completely, or in double freezer bags.

INGREDIENTS

Whole Milk – ¼ cup

Butter – 2 sticks, unsalted, room temperature

Sugar – ½ cup, granulated

Kosher Salt – ¾ teaspoon

Flour – 4½ cups

Yeast – 2 packets, active dry yeast (¼ ounce each)

Water – ¼ cup, hot tap water

Eggs – 6 extra-large, beaten

PREPARATION NOTES

Prep – Requires an over-night rise

Bake – 12 to 15 minutes

Yield – 2½ dozen brioche rolls

NOTES

_____

_____

_____

_____

_____

_____

_____

_____

Fresh Strawberry Preserves

THIS PRESERVE IS SO THICK AND LUXURIOUS IT IS ALMOST LIKE CANDY!

DIRECTIONS

Begin by cutting the green tops off all of the strawberries. Larger strawberries should be cut in half, leaving the smaller ones whole.

In a large heavy-bottomed sauce pan place the strawberries, blueberries, raspberries, apples, sugar, honey, and orange flavorings and toss until all the fruit is coated evenly.

Next, bring the mixture to a full boil over medium-high heat, stirring frequently. Keep the mixture at a full boil until the preserves reach 220 degrees F on a candy thermometer, roughly 30 to 40 minutes.

Once the preserves have reached the desired temperature, remove the pan from the heat and allow it to cool to room temperature.

Transfer to desired jars. The preserves will keep fresh in the refrigerator for up to 2 weeks.

INGREDIENTS

Strawberries – 3 pints, washed and drained

Sugar – 2¾ cups, super-fine

Honey – ½ cup

Orange Zest – 2 tablespoons, freshly zested

Orange Juice – 3 tablespoons, freshly squeezed

Granny Smith Apple – 1, peeled, cored, and cubed

Blueberries – ½ cup, washed and drained

Raspberries – ½ cup, washed and drained

PREPARATION NOTES

Yield – 4 cups

HERE'S AN IDEA

Fresh Strawberry Preserves are also the perfect topping to serve with my French Brioche Rolls (page 27). The recipe is so simple, it is sure to become a fast favorite!

NOTES

_____

_____

_____

_____

_____

_____

_____

_____

Gruyere & Thyme Popovers

AIRY, LIGHT, AND FILLED WITH FLAVOR

DIRECTIONS

Preheat oven to 400 degrees F and place a 6-cup popover pan in the bottom third of the oven while it is preheating.

In a small sauce pan, over medium heat, gently heat the milk to just below the simmering point. Remove from heat and set aside.

Next, sift the flour and salt into a small bowl.

In the bowl of an electric mixer, fitted with a whisk attachment and on medium speed, whisk the eggs until frothy, about 2 minutes.

Slowly add the warm milk to the whisked eggs. Then, with the mixer running on low speed, gradually add the flour and mix until smooth.

Add the fresh thyme and black pepper and mix just to incorporate.

Remove the popover pan from the oven and brush each cup with butter.

Fill all cups ¾ full with batter and sprinkle evenly with cheese.

Bake for 15 minutes, then rotate pan 180 degrees. Continue baking for an additional 30 minutes. Do not open the oven after rotating pans.

Once baked the popovers will have tripled in size and will be hollow. Invert the pan to remove the popovers and serve immediately.

INGREDIENTS

Whole Milk – 1½ cups

Flour – 1½ cups, all-purpose

Eggs – 3 extra-large

Kosher Salt – 2 teaspoons

Black Pepper – 1½ teaspoons

Fresh Thyme – 3 teaspoons

Gruyere Cheese – 3 ounces, grated

PREPARATION NOTES

Bake – 45 minutes

Yield – Serves 6

TRY THIS

Not only are these a fabulous addition to your morning menu, try pairing them with the Filet de Bœuf au Poivre (page 135) and a glass of Cabernet Sauvignon!

NOTES

_____

_____

_____

_____

_____

_____

_____

_____

Hello Neighbor Blueberry Muffins
YOU WILL BE THE ENVY OF THE BLOCK

DIRECTIONS

Preheat oven to 400 degrees F. Butter and flour a standard 12-well muffin pan, including the top surface.

In a small sauce pan set over low heat, combine the butter and milk. Once the butter is just melted remove the pan from the heat and set aside. Allow to sit at room temperature for 5 minutes, then whisk in the eggs and orange zest.

In a large mixing bowl, sift together the flour, granulated sugar, salt, nutmeg, and baking powder. Add the blueberries and toss to coat. Pour the milk mixture into the dry ingredients and fold gently until combined.

Using a 1¼-inch scoop, divide the batter evenly among the muffin pan wells. Sprinkle the tops with brown sugar.

Bake for 25 to 30 minutes, until golden brown.

Remove the muffin pan from the oven and place on a wire rack. Allow to cool for 10 minutes. Then, remove the muffins from the pan and serve warm.

To store or freeze the muffins allow to cool completely.

INGREDIENTS

Butter – 1½ sticks, unsalted, room temperature

Milk – 1½ cups, room temperature

Eggs – 3 extra-large

Orange Zest – 2 teaspoons, freshly zested

Flour – 3 cups, all-purpose

Sugar – $^2/_3$ cup, granulated

Baking Powder – 1 tablespoon

Kosher Salt – ¾ teaspoon

Nutmeg – $^1/_8$ teaspoon

Blueberries – 1½ cups, rinsed

Brown Sugar – $^1/_3$ cup, for garnish

PREPARATION NOTES

Bake – 25 to 30 minutes

Yield – Makes 12

HERE'S A TIP

To impress guests scoop the batter into the prepared muffin tins the night before. Cover and refrigerate until the next morning. Remove the pan and allow to sit at room temperature for 30 minutes before baking as instructed. Not only will it impress guests but the whole house will smell fabulous!

NOTES

_____

_____

_____

_____

_____

_____

_____

_____

Just Peachy Preserves
THE PERFECT ADDITION TO ANY BREAKFAST TABLE

DIRECTIONS

Start by slicing the unpeeled peaches in half and removing the pit. Cut each half into quarters. Do this for all 5 pounds of peaches. Remember, do not peel the peaches!

Next, combine the peach quarters, sugar, salt, honey, cardamom, lemon juice, and lemon zest in a large sauce pan.

Bring the mixture to a boil, stirring occasionally.

Lower the heat to medium-high and continue cooking for 40 to 45 minutes, scrapping down the sides of the pan and stirring occasionally.

Remove from the heat and let sit for 10 minutes.

Transfer to desired jars.

Your peach preserves will keep fresh in the refrigerator for up to 2 weeks.

INGREDIENTS

Peaches – 5 pounds, ripe

Sugar – 3½ cups, granulated

Honey – 3 tablespoons

Lemon Zest – 2 teaspoons, freshly zested

Lemon Juice – 2 tablespoons, freshly squeezed

Kosher Salt – ¼ teaspoon

Cardamom – $\frac{1}{8}$ teaspoon

PREPARATION NOTES

Yield – 4 cups

YUM!

Ryan loves peaches. Anything peaches! I could not fathom poaching and peeling 5 pounds of the delicious fruit. By keeping the skins on, my Just Peachy Preserves develop a deep amber color and a depth of flavor that delights the taste buds with an intensified subtlety.

HERE'S AN IDEA

Just Peachy Preserves also make a great topping for ice cream sundaes!

NOTES

_____
_____
_____
_____
_____
_____
_____
_____

Panko Brioche French Toast

A TWIST ON A CLASSIC BREAKFAST RECIPE

DIRECTIONS

Pre-heat oven to 200 degrees F.

Start by combining sliced strawberries, water, and 2 tablespoons of sugar in a medium bowl and set aside for 30 minutes.

While the strawberries are macerating, in a large bowl whisk together the half-and-half, eggs, vanilla, 4 tablespoons of sugar, cinnamon, nutmeg, and salt. Transfer the egg mixture into a large shallow plate or dish. Pour the panko into a separate large shallow plate or dish. Slice the brioche loaf into ¾-inch thick slices.

Heat 3 tablespoons of butter in a large sauté pan over low-medium heat.

Take a slice of brioche and dip it into the egg mixture, letting it soak for about 10 seconds on each side. Then, coat each side of the dipped brioche with the panko. Repeat with each slice of brioche until you have enough to fill the pan without over-crowding.

Place each slice into the sauté pan and cook for about 7 or 8 minutes on each side, or until nicely golden brown. When you flip the brioche, add another 2 tablespoons of butter into the pan. Place the cooked brioche onto a sheet pan and transfer into the oven to ensure they stay warm.

Wipe out the sauté pan with a paper towel, add another 3 tablespoons of butter and continue the same process until all brioche slices have been cooked.

Transfer the cooked brioche onto a large serving platter, drizzle with pure maple syrup, spoon on the strawberry mixture and dust with powdered sugar. Enjoy!

INGREDIENTS

Strawberries – 1 pint, ¼-inch sliced

Brioche – 1 loaf

Panko Bread Crumbs – 1½ cups

Sugar – 6 tablespoons, granulated, divided

Half-and-Half – 2 cups

Eggs – 8 extra-large, room temperature

Cinnamon – 2 tablespoons

Nutmeg – ¾ teaspoon

Vanilla – 2½ tablespoons, pure extract

Kosher Salt – ¾ teaspoon

Water – 2 tablespoons

Butter – 1 stick, unsalted, room temperature

Pure maple syrup – for serving guests

Powdered Sugar – As garnish

PREPARATION NOTES

Yield – 8 servings

A LITTLE STORY

Growing up, classic French toast was my breakfast of choice. My Nan always obliged and not only did she make it for me but for the rest of her grandchildren. Her recipe was simple yet full of flavor. I decided to turn up the flavor and add a crunchy and crispy outer layer with panko! It browns beautifully with the butter and adds that extra sumptuousness that makes breakfast worth getting out of bed.

HERE'S A TIP

Try serving this as a dessert with our Grand Marnier® Whipped Cream (page 187) as a fabulous topping!

NOTES

_____

_____

_____

_____

_____

_____

_____

_____

_____

Pretzel White Chocolate Pancakes

THESE PANCAKES WILL CURB THAT SALTY AND SWEET CRAVING!

DIRECTIONS

Preheat oven to 200 degrees F.

Start by melting the chocolate, 2 tablespoons of half-and-half, and 1½ teaspoons of vanilla in a double boiler over low heat until melted, stirring frequently. Remove from the heat and set aside in a serving pitcher.

Then, mix the caramel sauce and 2 tablespoons of half-and-half in a small bowl until well combined. Set aside in a serving pitcher.

Combine the flour, salt, brown sugar, baking powder, and baking soda in a large bowl. Then add the eggs, buttermilk, 2½ teaspoons of vanilla, and ¼ cup of melted butter. Whisk together until the batter is smooth.

Add 1¼ cups of crushed pretzels to the batter and stir until well combined.

Next, heat 2 tablespoons of butter in a large sauté pan over medium heat.

Using a ¼ measuring cup, scoop even amounts of the batter into the sauté pan (being careful to keep them from touching) and let each pancake cook for 3 to 5 minutes on each side, or until golden brown. (The top of the pancakes will form bubbles and that generally means they are ready to flip.)

Place the cooked pancakes onto a sheet pan and transfer into the oven to keep them warm while you cook the remaining pancakes.

After each batch of pancakes carefully wipe out the sauté pan (it's hot!) with a paper towel, add another 2 tablespoons of butter and continue the same process until all pancake batter is used.

Let your guests drizzle the desired amount of white chocolate and caramel sauce onto their pancakes. Top with more crushed pretzels, and enjoy!

INGREDIENTS

Flour – 2 cups, all-purpose

Brown Sugar – ⅓ cup

Kosher Salt – ¾ teaspoon, plus more for garnish

Baking Soda – 1 teaspoon

Baking Powder – 2¼ teaspoons

Buttermilk – 2½ cups

Eggs – 2 extra-large, beaten

Vanilla – 4 teaspoons, pure extract, divided

Butter – 1 stick, unsalted, divided

Salted Pretzels – 2 cups, crushed, divided

Fleur de Sel Caramel Sauce – 10 ounces, good store-bought salted caramel

White Chocolate – 8 ounces, chopped

Half-and-Half – 4 tablespoons, divided

PREPARATION NOTES

Yield – 12 pancakes

A LITTLE STORY

Friends were visiting from Iowa and I wanted to make them a very special and unique breakfast. One friend liked white chocolate and the other loved pretzels. After testing and eating, and testing some more, I created this absolutely decadent dish. The crunchy pretzels with the puffy pancakes balance the salt and sweetness from the caramel and white chocolate. Your taste buds will wake up and thank you!

NOTES

Salmon Tartine

CHIC, EASY TO MAKE, AND EASY TO EAT!

DIRECTIONS

In small glass bowl add the mascarpone, butter, Dijon mustard, whole grain mustard, and dill. With a spatula combine thoroughly until well blended and smooth.

Toast 4 large slices of hearty bread. While still warm, spread half of the creamed mixture onto each slice. Sprinkle half of the capers onto each slice and season with the salt.

Flake 2 ounces of smoked or cured salmon onto each piece of toast. Season with freshly cracked pepper. Cut each slice in half and arrange on a plate to serve.

INGREDIENTS

Honey Rustic Bread – 4 large slices, toasted

Salmon (smoked or cured) – 8 ounces

Capers – 3 tablespoons, drained

Mascarpone – 4 tablespoons

Butter – 2 tablespoons

Dijon Mustard – 2 teaspoons

Whole Grain Mustard – 2 teaspoons

Dill – ½ teaspoon, fresh

Coarse Salt – ½ teaspoon

Black Pepper – ½ teaspoon, freshly cracked

PREPARATION NOTES

Yield – Serves 4

HERE'S A TIP

You can use either smoked salmon or cured salmon, depending on your preference. The Salmon Tartine is a great small-plate option for any breakfast or brunch. The recipe can be easily doubled or tripled to serve more guests.

NOTES

_____

_____

_____

_____

_____

_____

_____

_____

_____

The Ultimate Benedict

AN OVER-THE-TOP DISH WORTH THE STOVE-TOP LOGISTICS

DIRECTIONS

Preheat the oven to 400 degrees F. Place the bacon strips evenly spaced on a wire rack set in a sheet pan. Bake for 20 to 25 minutes, until browned and crispy. Flip once half way through the baking time. Then, set aside on a paper towel-lined plate.

Hollandaise Sauce
First, in a 12-inch sauté pan, melt 1 stick of butter. Set aside and let cool.

Separate the egg yolks into a large glass bowl. Add the lemon juice and whisk briskly until the yolks are thick and luxurious. They should double in volume and will be a pale yellow.

Place the bowl over a saucepan of gently simmering water. Be careful that the water in the saucepan does not touch the bottom of the bowl.

Next, slowly pour the melted butter into the bowl while continuing to whisk. Add the cayenne pepper, salt, and black pepper. As you whisk, the mixture will thicken and double in volume again.

Remove from the heat and cover tightly. Set aside in a warm place.

Eggs Benedict
Spinach—In the same sauté pan used to melt the butter, melt 1½ tablespoons of butter over medium heat. Once hot, add the garlic and lightly sauté for 1 to 2 minutes. Add the spinach leaves directly to the pan. Toss in the butter and garlic, add the salt, and gently fold and stir as the leaves wilt and sauté, for about 3 to 4 minutes. Transfer the spinach to a small bowl, cover tightly, and set aside in a warm place.

Fried Tomatoes—Thoroughly pat dry 4 tomato slices. In the same sauté pan used to sauté the spinach, melt ½ tablespoon of butter over medium-high heat. Once hot, place the 4 slices of tomato in the sauté pan. Pan-fry the tomato slices for 3

English Muffins—Slice the English Muffins in half and toast to a golden brown.

Poached Eggs—In the same saucepan used for the Hollandaise Sauce, increase the heat to bring the water to a gentle boil. Add the vinegar to the water. Next, using a wooden spoon, stir the water vigorously to create a small "whirlpool". This will help the egg whites to stay together as one mass. Carefully crack an egg into the vortex of the swirling water. Be careful not to break the yolk. Do the same for the other three eggs. Poach for 4 minutes, or until the egg whites are set and the yolk is still soft. Remove the eggs gently from the water with a slotted spoon.

Assembly—Place one English Muffin half on a plate, cut side up. Place a pan-fried tomato slice on the English Muffin. Spoon ¼ of the spinach and garlic mixture onto the tomato. Break one strip of bacon in half and place crisscross on the spinach. Gently place a poached egg on the bacon. Spoon ¼ of the Hollandaise sauce over the egg. If the Hollandaise sauce thickens too much as it rested whisk in a splash of hot water to thin. Garnish with a dash of hot paprika and cracked black pepper to taste. Repeat with the 3 remaining English muffins.

INGREDIENTS

Hollandaise Sauce

Egg Yolks – 4 extra-large

Butter – 1 stick, unsalted

Lemon Juice – 1½ tablespoons

Cayenne Pepper – ½ teaspoon

Kosher Salt – ½ teaspoon

Black Pepper – ½ teaspoon, freshly cracked

Eggs Benedict

Eggs – 4 large

English Muffins – 2, cut in half

Vinegar – 1 tablespoon

Butter – 2 tablespoons, divided

Garlic – 2 cloves, minced

Baby Spinach Leaves – 6 ounces, pre-washed

Bacon – 4 strips, thick-cut

Kosher Salt – ½ teaspoon

Black Pepper – 1 teaspoon, freshly cracked

Tomato – 1 medium-sized, ½-inch sliced

Hot Paprika – For garnish

PREPARATION NOTES

Yield – Serves 4

You'll Go Bananas Bread

JUST AS BANANAS FOR BREAKFAST OR WITH A SCOOP OF ICE CREAM FOR DESSERT

DIRECTIONS

Preheat oven to 350 degrees F.

Lightly butter and flour a 9x5 inch loaf pan and set aside.

In a small bowl combine raisins and hot water for 10 minutes to rehydrate, then drain and set aside.

Next, in a medium bowl sift together flour, baking soda, baking powder, salt, and cinnamon.

In the bowl of an electric mixer fitted with a paddle attachment, cream together the butter and sugar on medium speed until light and fluffy, about 5 minutes.

On low speed add the eggs one at a time to the creamed butter and sugar mixture. Then add the vanilla, honey, raisins, and bananas. Continue to mix until all the ingredients are just incorporated. The wet mixture should have pieces of banana visible in the batter.

Next, with the mixer on low speed, slowly add the flour into the wet ingredients, until just incorporated. Then pour the batter into the prepared loaf pan and sprinkle the top with 3 tablespoons of brown sugar.

Transfer the pan into the oven and bake for 60 to 70 minutes, or until a toothpick inserted into the center of the loaf comes out clean.

Allow the loaf to cool in the pan for 10 minutes, and then turn out onto a wire rack to finish cooling completely. Slice to the desired thickness and serve hot, or room temperature.

INGREDIENTS

Flour – 2 cups, all-purpose

Baking Powder – 1 teaspoon

Baking Soda – 1 teaspoon

Kosher Salt – ½ teaspoon

Cinnamon – 2 teaspoons

Brown Sugar – ¾ cup, plus 3 tablespoons for garnish

Raisins – ¾ cup

Eggs – 2 extra-large, room temperature

Butter – 1 stick, unsalted, room temperature

Vanilla – 2 teaspoons, pure extract

Bananas – 4 over-ripe, peeled and halved

Honey – 3 tablespoons

Water – 3 tablespoons, hot

PREPARATION NOTES

Bake – 60 to 70 minutes

Yield – 1 loaf

A LITTLE TIP

Using very ripe bananas is what gives my banana bread its intense flavor. You can also add ½ cup of walnuts to the recipe at the end. Just make sure you toss them in a little bit of flour beforehand so they will not sink to the bottom of the batter in the pan.

NOTES

_____

_____

_____

_____

_____

_____

_____

_____

_____

Starters & Salads

EASY RECIPES TO START THINGS OFF RIGHT

Big Bruschetta with Gorgonzola

BUTTERY BREAD AND BOLD GORGONZOLA WILL MAKE THIS A FAVORITE!

DIRECTIONS

Preheat oven to 350 degrees F.

Combine butter, garlic, 2 tablespoons of olive oil, salt, and pepper in a small bowl and mix together.

Slice the baguette into approximately 28 ½-inch thick pieces and spread the butter mixture evenly onto each piece.

Line a sheet pan with parchment paper and arrange the buttered slices of baguette and bake for 15 minutes.

Remove the sheet pan from the oven and top each slice with an even amount of tomatoes. Then, drizzle with the remaining 2 tablespoons of olive oil and top with crumbled Gorgonzola cheese.

Return the sheet pan back to the oven and bake for an additional 7 to 9 minutes, or until the Gorgonzola is slightly melted.

Remove the sheet pan carefully from the oven and sprinkle with dried oregano.

Garnish with more salt and pepper to taste and serve hot.

INGREDIENTS

Baguette – 1 large loaf, sliced ½-inch thick (28 pieces)

Butter – 6 tablespoons, unsalted, room temperature

Garlic – 4 cloves, minced

Kosher Salt – ¾ teaspoon

Black Pepper – ¾ teaspoon, freshly cracked

Olive Oil – 4 tablespoons, divided

Heirloom Grape Tomatoes – 12 ounces, quartered

Gorgonzola (Italian) – 5 ounces, crumbled

Oregano – 2 teaspoons, dried

PREPARATION NOTES

Bake – 25 minutes

Serves – 6 to 8 people

A TASTY IDEA

Garlic bread meets gorgonzola in my version of a bruschetta! Topped with fresh tomatoes and lots of pepper, Big Bruschetta with Gorgonzola is great to serve as part of a lunch, as an appetizer, or along with dinner!

NOTES

_____

_____

_____

_____

_____

_____

_____

_____

_____

Caprese Lollipop

THESE BITE-SIZED SAVORY TREATS ARE PERFECT FOR ANY PARTY

DIRECTIONS

Start by choosing a serving platter with at least a ¼-inch lip.

Coat the bottom of the dish with a thin layer of olive oil and sprinkle evenly with salt and pepper.

Skewer a mini tomato, rolled basil leaf, and a mozzarella ball onto a cocktail pick and set aside. Repeat the same process until all 30 lollipops have been assembled.

Arrange the Caprese Lollipops on the serving platter.

Serve at room temperature.

INGREDIENTS

Basil – 30 small leaves

Tomatoes – 30 mini, heirloom or grape

Mozzarella – 30 bocconcini (small bite-sized balls)

Olive Oil – 1/3 cup

Kosher Salt – 1 tablespoon

Black Pepper – 1 tablespoon

Wooden Picks – 30 wooden picks

PREPARATION NOTES

Yield – Serves 10

HERE'S AN IDEA

The lollipops can be made ahead of time and stored in an air tight container overnight in the refrigerator. Plate 30 minutes before guests arrive and the lollipops will be the perfect temperature!

NOTES

_____

_____

_____

_____

_____

_____

_____

_____

_____

Craquelins Savoureux

THESE SAVORY CRACKERS INCLUDE A WONDERFUL CHOCOLATY SURPRISE

DIRECTIONS

Simply layer each cracker with a slice of Gruyere, a basil leaf, a dollop of honey (about the size of a nickel), and topped with a piece of dark chocolate.

Arrange on a serving platter or flat board.

Easily expand the recipe as needed.

INGREDIENTS

Gruyere Cheese – 6 ounces, cut into 30 thin slices

Dark Chocolate – 3 ounces, rough chopped

Basil – 30 small fresh leaves

Water Crackers – 30, plain

Honey – In a squeezable container

PREPARATION NOTES

Yield – Serves 10

A LITTLE TIP

Meaning "savory crackers" in French, this quick and easy-to-assemble no-cook appetizer is perfect to bring to a party. Simply prepare all of the ingredients in advance, pack them all in to-go containers, and assemble at the party!

A TASTY IDEA

Serve these Craquelins with a glass of port to finish a meal. An unexpected twist on dessert!

NOTES

Farfalle Skewers with Meatballs

A FUN AND EASY-TO-EAT APPETIZER

DIRECTIONS

Start by gently heating Marc's Home-Style Tuscan Tomato Sauce (page 143) in a sauce pan over low-medium heat, allowing it to simmer for about 10 minutes. Remove from the heat and set aside.

Meanwhile, cook the vegetarian meatballs according to package directions. For even more flavor cook the meatballs in the sauce. Set aside.

Bring a pot of well-salted water to a boil and cook the farfalle according to package directions. Drain the pasta and set aside.

On a serving platter ladle the tomato sauce in the bottom of the dish.

Assemble each wooden pick with a piece of farfalle and then a vegetarian meatball. Continue this process for the rest of the picks.

Place each skewer with the meatball side down and sprinkle with parmesan, salt and pepper to taste.

Serve warm or at room temperature.

INGREDIENTS

Vegetarian Meatballs – 30 meatballs, Quorn® brand recommended

Marc's Home-Style Tuscan Tomato Sauce – 3 cups (page 143)

Farfalle – 30 pieces, cooked to al dente

Parmesan Cheese – 1 cup, freshly grated

Kosher Salt – To taste, for garnish

Black Pepper – To taste, for garnish

Wooden Picks – 30 skewers

PREPARATION NOTES

Yield – Serves 10

FOOD FOR THOUGHT

I prefer to assemble these in small batches on white heat-proof plates and keep them warm in a 200 degree F oven. You can also create this dish using your favorite family meatball recipe. My vegetarian version always pleasantly surprises our non-vegetarian guests and provides a wonderful meatless option that everyone will enjoy.

NOTES

Goat Cheese with Cracked Pepper & Herbs

HERBS AND SPICES ARE THE PERFECT COMPLEMENT TO CREAMY GOAT CHEESE

DIRECTIONS

Start by mixing the fresh herbs, salt, and pepper in a small bowl. Transfer the mixture to a shallow dish.

Slice the goat cheese into 6 equal-sized portions.

Press each of the goat cheese medallions into the herbed mixture to evenly coat all sides.

Arrange onto the serving board and serve with your favorite crackers.

You can store the goat cheese medallions in an air-tight container in the refrigerator for up to 3 days.

INGREDIENTS

Goat Cheese – 7 ounces

Kosher Salt – ¾ teaspoon

Black Pepper – 1 teaspoon

Thyme – ¼ cup, freshly minced

Rosemary – ¼ cup, freshly mined

Dill – 2 tablespoons, freshly minced

Parsley – ¼ cup, freshly minced

Chives – ¼ cup, freshly minced

PREPARATION NOTES

Yield – Serves 6

A QUICK TIP

This is a fantastic savory starter to serve as part of a cheese board or antipasti platter.

NOTES

Green Pea Guacamole
A FRESH AND BRIGHT VARIATION OF A CLASSIC APPETIZER

DIRECTIONS

Simply add all of the ingredients to the bowl of a food processor fitted with a steel blade and pulse 8 to 10 times, until chopped and mixed, but not completely puréed. The green pea guacamole should have a chunky texture.

INGREDIENTS

Peas – 2 (15-ounce) cans, sweet peas, well drained

Garlic – 3 cloves, rough chopped

Red Onion – 1 small, cut into 8 pieces

Jalapeño – 1 small, seeded and roughly chopped

Lime Juice – 1 medium-sized, freshly squeezed

Kosher Salt – ½ teaspoon

Black Pepper – ¾ teaspoon

Cilantro – $\frac{1}{3}$ cup, whole leaves

Grape Tomatoes – ¾ cup, cut in quarters

Hot Sauce – 8 to 10 dashes

PREPARATION NOTES

Yield – 3 cups

REMEMBER THIS

The guacamole will become slightly watery after sitting for a bit. Simply stir with a spoon on occasion to keep it well mixed. Green Pea Guacamole also tastes great when used as a sandwich spread!

NOTES

Grissini

HOMEMADE BREAD STICKS MADE EASY

DIRECTIONS

Start by dissolving the yeast, sugar and water in a small bowl. Allow to sit in a warm place for 10 minutes.

Meanwhile, sift the flour, salt and pepper into a large bowl. Add the yeast mixture and olive oil and stir to combine.

Turn the dough out onto a lightly floured surface and knead for 10 minutes.

Place the dough into a lightly oiled bowl and cover with plastic wrap. Place the dough in a warm place for 1 hour, until doubled in size.

Preheat the oven to 450 degrees F. Line two sheet pans with parchment paper.

Using your fist, punch the dough at the center to expel the gases. Remove from the bowl and add the basil, garlic, and Parmesan. Knead for 1 minute to fully incorporate.

Using a pastry knife (or simply a large knife) divide the dough into 24 equal portions by dividing the dough ball in half, and then halving each piece until you have 24 equally sized pieces. Roll each portion into a 12-inch long stick. Place onto the prepared pans side by side. Brush the tops with butter.

Bake for 15 minutes, or until they are crisp and golden brown.

Remove the grissini from the pan and let cool on a wire rack.

Serve either warm or at room temperature. Grissini may be stored for 3 to 4 days in an airtight container.

A TASTY IDEA

Not only do these grissini taste amazingly, they can also be an edible table decoration for an Italian-themed dinner party. Arrange them standing up in cleaned empty tomato cans to add whimsy to your next dinner!

INGREDIENTS

Flour – 4 cups, all-purpose

Sugar – 1 teaspoon

Olive Oil – 3 tablespoons

Garlic – 6 cloves, finely minced

Basil – 1 cup, freshly chopped

Parmesan Cheese – $1/3$ cup, freshly grated

Kosher Salt – ¾ teaspoon

Black Pepper – 1 teaspoon

Butter – 2 tablespoons, unsalted, room temperature

Yeast (active dry) – ¼ ounce, equal to 1 packet

Water – 1¼ cups, warm

PREPARATION NOTES

Bake – 15 minutes

Yield – Makes 24

NOTES

_____

_____

_____

_____

_____

_____

_____

_____

_____

Henrietta's Deviled Eggs
ALWAYS A FINGER-FRIENDLY PARTY FAVORITE

DIRECTIONS

For the perfect hard-boiled eggs, start by bringing a large sauce pan of water to a rolling boil over high heat.

Add the room temperature eggs to the boiling water and cook for exactly 12 minutes.

Remove the eggs from boiling water with a slotted spoon and plunge into an ice water bath. Let the cooked eggs sit in the cold water for about 20 minutes or until cool enough to handle.

With a light pressure roll the cooled eggs on the countertop to break the shell and simply peel away. Rinse gently under cool water to ensure all of the egg shell bits are off of the cooked egg. You will have a perfectly cooked hard-boiled egg every time!

To devil the eggs, carefully cut each egg in half lengthwise and gently remove the cooked yolk setting aside in a separate bowl. Be very careful not to rip or tear the cooked egg white as it will be part of your final display.

Place all of the yolks into the bowl of an electric mixer fitted with a whisk attachment. Add the mayonnaise, both mustards, salt, black pepper, crushed red pepper flakes, turmeric, cardamom, lemon zest, and lemon juice.

With the mixer on medium speed blend all of the ingredients until the mixture is smooth and the yolks have all been incorporated.

Fill each empty egg white half with a rounded tablespoon of the filling. Repeat this step until all the egg halves have been filled.

Arrange the eggs on a serving platter and garnish with fresh thyme leaves. Serve at room temperature.

INGREDIENTS

Eggs – 8 extra-large, room temperature

Mayonnaise – 5 tablespoons

Whole Grain Mustard – 1 teaspoon

Dijon Mustard – 1 teaspoon

Pepper – ½ teaspoon, freshly cracked

Kosher Salt – $\frac{1}{8}$ teaspoon

Crushed Red Pepper Flakes – $\frac{1}{8}$ teaspoon

Turmeric – $\frac{1}{8}$ teaspoon

Cardamom – $\frac{1}{8}$ teaspoon

Lemon Zest – ½ teaspoon, freshly zested

Lemon Juice – 1 teaspoon, freshly squeezed

Fresh Thyme – 2 teaspoons, as garnish

PREPARATION NOTES

Serves – 6 to 8 people

A LITTLE STORY

During the summer of 2011 Ryan and I spent time visiting family on their farm. Fresh eggs were plentiful from the hens that were on the property. One hen, Henrietta, took a liking to me after I helped her free herself from being trapped under a fence. Not only did I glitter her wings and carry her around like a puppy, but I also created a dish in her honor! Henrietta would approve. (And I have since traded carrying around Henrietta with our sweet pup Lady.)

NOTES

Marinated Artichoke Hearts

SERVE WITH DRINKS, AS PART OF AN ANTIPASTI PLATTER, IN A SALAD OR PASTA DISH

DIRECTIONS

Start by whisking together the garlic, oil, spices, lemon, and herbs in a medium-sized bowl.

Add the artichokes to the mixture and toss well to coat evenly. Cover with plastic wrap and refrigerate overnight.

Serve at room temperature.

INGREDIENTS

Artichoke Hearts – 14 ounces, canned hearts, well drained

Olive Oil – ½ cup

Dill – 2 tablespoons, freshly chopped

Parsley – 3 tablespoons, freshly chopped

Basil – 2 tablespoons, freshly chopped

Lemon – 2 tablespoons lemon juice and zest

Crushed Red Pepper Flakes – ¼ teaspoon

Kosher Salt – ½ teaspoon

Black Pepper – ½ teaspoon

Garlic – 3 cloves, finely minced

PREPARATION NOTES

Yield – Serves 6

HERE'S A TIP

These Marinated Artichoke Hearts are perfect as part of a picnic. Pack them in Chinese take-out containers and bring disposable chopsticks. No cleanup!

NOTES

Parmesan Crisps

THESE ARE THE RAVE IN BISTRO DINING GARNISHES! BE CHIC AND JOIN THE PARTY!

DIRECTIONS

Preheat oven to 400 degrees F.

Place 1/8 cup of Parmigiano-Reggiano onto a parchment-lined baking sheet and lightly pat down into a circle. Repeat with the remaining cheese, leaving 1-inch of space between each circle.

Bake for 6 to 7 minutes, or until golden and crisp. Allow to cool on the baking sheet before transferring.

INGREDIENTS

Parmigiano-Reggiano Cheese – 2 cups, freshly grated

PREPARATION NOTES

Bake – 6 to 7 minutes

Yield – Makes 16 crisps

A TASTY IDEA

Before baking, try sprinkling with a little freshly-cracked black pepper for a savory twist. Serve these with a glass of champagne before dinner or as a delicious edible garnish for the Caesar Salad with Hearts of Romaine (page 79).

NOTES

_____

_____

_____

_____

_____

_____

_____

_____

Roasted & Spiced Nuts

SERVE WITH A SIGNATURE COCKTAIL TO START THE PARTY OFF RIGHT

DIRECTIONS

Preheat oven to 350 degrees F.

In a large bowl combine nuts, oil, honey, lime juice, paprika, black pepper, red pepper flakes, 1 teaspoon of salt, 2 tablespoons of rosemary, and 1 tablespoon of thyme.

Toss to coat nuts evenly and spread onto a sheet pan.

Roast for 20 to 25 minutes, tossing twice during the baking process.

Remove the sheet pan from the oven and sprinkle with the remaining salt, thyme, and rosemary. While the nuts are cooling on the sheet pan toss occasionally to prevent them from sticking together.

Serve warm.

INGREDIENTS

Raw Almonds – 2 cups

Raw Pecans – 2 cups

Raw Cashews – 2 cups

Vegetable Oil – ¼ cup

Honey – ¼ cup

Lime – 1 medium-sized, juiced

Black Pepper – 2 teaspoons

Hot Paprika – 2 teaspoons

Red Pepper Flakes – ½ teaspoon

Kosher Salt – 2 teaspoons, divided

Rosemary – 4 tablespoons, freshly minced, divided

Thyme – 2 tablespoons, freshly minced, divided

PREPARATION NOTES

Bake – 20 to 25 minutes

Yield – 6 cups

REMEMBER THIS

Roasted Spiced Nuts may be stored in an air tight container for up to 1 week. If you make this yummy cocktail snack ahead of time just spread on a parchment paper-lined sheet span to warm in a 200 degree F oven for 5 minutes just before serving.

NOTES

_____

_____

_____

_____

_____

_____

_____

_____

Sautéed Onion & Cream Cheese Dip

DO NOT PLAN ON HAVING ANY OF THIS CREAMY DIP LEFT OVER

DIRECTIONS

Preheat oven to 350 degrees F.

Start by heating the olive oil over medium heat in a 12-inch sauté pan.

Once the oil is hot, add onions, salt, and pepper. Sauté until tender and translucent, about 10 minutes.

Add the garlic and continue to sauté for an additional 1 to 2 minutes, enough to cook off the bite of the garlic but careful not to burn.

Turn heat to low, add the cheeses, basil, and thyme. Continue to cook, stirring occasionally until all the ingredients are incorporated.

Pour the mixture into a small casserole dish and bake, covered, for 30 minutes.

Uncover, and bake for an additional 10 minutes, until bubbly!

Remove from the oven, and serve with sliced baguette or water crackers.

INGREDIENTS

Olive Oil – 3 tablespoons

Yellow Onions – 2 large, yellow, ¼-inch dice

Cream Cheese – 8 ounces, room temperature

Mascarpone Cheese – 8 ounces, room temperature

Basil – ¼ cup, rough chopped

Thyme – 3 tablespoons, fresh, minced

Kosher Salt – ½ teaspoon

Black Pepper – 1 teaspoon

Garlic – 3 cloves, minced

Parmesan Cheese – ¼ cup, freshly grated

PREPARATION NOTES

Bake – 40 minutes

Yield – Serves 8 people

A LITTLE TIP

For a little heat add ½ teaspoon (or more if you dare) of crushed red pepper flakes while you are sautéing the onions!

NOTES

_____

_____

_____

_____

_____

_____

_____

_____

_____

_____

Savory Tomato Tartlet

THESE TARTLETS ARE GREAT RIGHT FROM THE OVEN OR AT ROOM TEMPERATURE

DIRECTIONS

Preheat the oven to 400 degrees F.

Place the 6 tomato halves cut-side up onto a sheet pan and drizzle with 3 tablespoons of olive oil, the balsamic vinegar, and 1 teaspoon each of salt and black pepper. Place into the oven and roast for 45 minutes. Remove from the oven and set aside.

Raise the oven temperature to 450 degrees F.

Meanwhile, in a 12-inch sauté pan, heat the olive oil over medium heat. Add the onions, sugar, 1 teaspoon each of salt and black pepper, and the red pepper flakes. Stir well and cook for 10 minutes.

Next, add the garlic and continue to cook for another 2 minutes. Remove from the heat and set aside.

Roll out the defrosted puff pastry dough, to about ¼-inch thick, on a lightly floured surface.

Using a small sharp knife cut out 6 circles of dough, 5 inches in diameter. Place each circle side by side on a parchment-lined sheet pan and brush the circles evenly with the beaten egg yolk.

Assemble each tart by placing 1 teaspoon of pesto in the center of each circle and spread it evenly, leaving a ½-inch border at the edge.

Divide the onion mixture evenly among each circle and place a dollop in the center of the circle with an evenly divided amount of capers and olive quarters. Top with a tomato half, cut side up, and shaving of cheese.

Bake for 15 minutes, or until puffed and golden brown. Sprinkle with salt and pepper to taste.

INGREDIENTS

Plum Tomatoes – 3 large, cut in half lengthwise

Yellow Onions – 2 large, thinly sliced

Garlic – 6 cloves, minced

Kosher Salt – 2 teaspoons, divided

Black Pepper – 2 teaspoons, divided

Sugar – 2 tablespoons, granulated

Crushed Red Pepper Flakes – $\frac{1}{8}$ teaspoon

Capers – 30 capers, well drained

Pesto – 6 teaspoons

Puff Pastry Dough – 3 sheets, thawed following package directions

Parmesan Cheese – 6 large shavings

Olives – 6 olives, quartered

Olive Oil – 6 tablespoons, divided

Balsamic Vinegar – 2 tablespoons

Eggs – 1 yolk, beaten

PREPARATION NOTES

Bake – 15 minutes

Yield – Makes 6 tarts

NOTES

_____

_____

_____

_____

_____

_____

_____

_____

The Cheese Platter

A BEAUTIFUL NO-COOK ENTERTAINING OPTION THAT IS EASY TO ASSEMBLE

DIRECTIONS

Assembling a cheese board is simple and can make a big impact on a food table or set out in the living room while your guests are enjoying a glass of wine or champagne.

Start by choosing 4 to 5 different cheeses of different types. Ask the cheese monger at your favorite market for a sample and try new flavors. A few of my favorites are listed to the right.

Most cheeses taste best at room temperature and should not be served straight from the refrigerator. Allow the cheeses to come to room temperature. Place the cheeses on a large wooden board, leaving a small space between each selection. Always serve each cheese with its own small cheese knife.

Next, choose in-season fruit. Strawberries and blueberries are reliable standards. Not only do they add beautiful color, but they also pair well with many cheeses. Arrange the fruit in separate bowls or on small plates and place directly onto the board.

The addition of preserves always makes for interesting flavor combinations. Fig preserves, or even a red-pepper jelly, are exotic and fun flavors for your guests to experiment with safely. Savory preserves work better for a cheese board. Leave the grape jelly for the kiddie's lunchbox!

Lastly, arrange thin slices of fresh baguette and a selection of crackers. A good host should always buy more crackers than they think they will need!

INGREDIENTS

Cheese Options

Stilton (Blue Cheese)

Manchego (aged 12 months)

Smoked Gouda

English Cheddar

Swiss Gruyere

Camembert (similar to Brie)

Herbed Goat Cheese

Parmigiano-Reggiano

Pecorino Romano

PREPARATION NOTES

Yield – Serves 8 to 10

FOOD FOR THOUGHT

Be creative! This is a fabulous time to try cheeses in small amounts that you may never have tried before. You can always use the left-over cheese in one of the fabulous recipes in this cookbook!

A GOOD IDEA

Keep the labels. At least one of your guests will ask about your selections and it can be easy to forget, especially if you are trying new cheeses. After your soirée you will be able to remember which ones to buy again!

NOTES

_____

_____

_____

_____

_____

_____

_____

Tomato & Goat Cheese Crostata

AN ELEGANT AND TRULY DELICIOUS DISH FOR BRUNCH OR LUNCH

DIRECTIONS

Preheat oven to 350 degrees F.

In the bowl of a food processor fitted with a steel blade, add the flour, butter, sugar, white pepper, and ½ teaspoon salt. Pulse the food processor 10 times or until the butter is the size of small peas. Add the grated cheddar and pulse another 2 times.

Next, with the food processor running, slowly add the cold water down the feed tube, adding just enough for the dough to come together into a single mass. Turn the mixture out onto a floured surface and quickly shape into a ball. Cover the dough ball in plastic wrap and refrigerate for 30 minutes.

Once chilled, roll out the pastry dough onto a lightly floured surface. Form into a 14-inch circle, ¼-inch thick. Transfer the dough to a parchment-covered sheet pan. Brush the pastry disc evenly with half of the beaten egg yolk and sprinkle with the breadcrumbs.

Arrange the sliced tomatoes on the pastry so that they overlap, leaving a 2-inch border from the edge. Crumble on the goat cheese and sprinkle with ½ teaspoon of salt, and the black pepper.

Next, turn the edge of the pastry in over the tomatoes, pleating the dough. The center of the Crostata will be exposed. Brush the remaining egg yolk on the pleated pastry.

Bake for 40 to 45 minutes, or until golden brown. Remove from the oven, drizzle with olive oil, and garnish with basil leaves. Season with more salt and pepper to taste.

Serve either warm or at room temperature.

INGREDIENTS

Flour – 1½ cups, all-purpose

Butter – 1 stick, unsalted, very cold, diced

English Cheddar – 3 tablespoons, grated

Water – 8 tablespoons, iced

Kosher Salt – 1 teaspoon, divided

White Pepper – ½ teaspoon

Sugar – 2 teaspoons, granulated

Eggs – 1 yolk, beaten

Bread Crumbs – 3 tablespoons, plain

Roma Tomatoes – 5 medium-sized, ¼-inch sliced

Goat Cheese – 3½ ounces

Black Pepper – 1 teaspoon

Olive Oil – 1 tablespoon

Basil – 5 to 7 small leaves, as garnish

PREPARATION NOTES

Bake – 40 to 45 minutes

Yield – Serves 6

NOTES

ANOTHER IDEA

You can also make this with heirloom tomatoes or tomatoes that have been ripened on the vine. Whatever looks (and smells) the best at the farmer's market or grocer!

Caesar Salad with Hearts of Romaine

THIS HOME-MADE UPDATE IS BETTER THAN THE ORIGINAL

DIRECTIONS

In a small sauté pan heat ½ cup olive oil over medium-high heat. Once the oil is hot, add the smashed cloves of garlic and cook for 5 minutes. Remove from the heat and set aside to cool.

In the bowl of a food processor, fitted with a steel blade, add the lemon zest, lemon juice, Dijon mustard, anchovy paste, Worchester sauce, salt, black pepper, champagne vinegar, egg yolks, and olive oil, including the smashed garlic.

Pulse the food processer to combine, and then run continuously for 2 minutes.

Next, add the parmesan cheese to the food process bowl and run continuously for 1 minute. While the food processor is running, pour the water down the feed tube and run for another 5 minutes or until the mixture is creamy and smooth.

Cut the white stalk end off of the romaine and separate the leaves. Wash under cold water to remove any dirt near the base of the leaves. Dry thoroughly.

Arrange 3 to 4 large leaves on a plate. Drizzle with the Caesar dressing and season with a pinch of salt and black pepper.

INGREDIENTS

Romaine – 1 large whole heart

Egg Yolks – 2 extra-large

Garlic – 6 cloves, smashed

Olive Oil – ½ cup

Lemon Zest – ½ of a lemon, freshly zested

Lemon Juice – 3 teaspoons, freshly squeezed

Dijon Mustard – 2 teaspoons

Anchovy Paste – 3 teaspoons

Parmesan Cheese – ½ cup, grated

Worchester Sauce – 1½ teaspoons

Coarse Salt – 2 teaspoons

Black Pepper – 2 teaspoons, freshly cracked

Champagne Vinegar – 2 teaspoons

Water – ¼ cup, room temperature

PREPARATION NOTES

Yield – Serves 6

Yield – 1½ cups of dressing

NOTES

_____

_____

_____

_____

_____

_____

_____

_____

_____

Watermelon & Goat Cheese Salad

THIS BRIGHT AND COLORFUL SALAD IS PERFECT FOR SUMMER ENTERTAINING

DIRECTIONS

Start by arranging the arugula onto a large serving platter.

Place the watermelon wedges overlapping down the center of the platter.

Crumble and evenly distribute the goat cheese, onion, salt, pepper, and basil.

Drizzle the entire salad with olive oil and balsamic vinegar.

Serve immediately.

INGREDIENTS

Watermelon – 12 wedges, ½-inch thick

Arugula – 10 ounces

Red Onion – 1 small, thinly sliced

Goat Cheese – 6 ounces, crumbled

Basil – ½ cup, thinly chopped

Kosher Salt – 2 teaspoon

Black Pepper – 2 teaspoons

Olive Oil – 3 tablespoons

Balsamic Vinegar – 3 tablespoons

PREPARATION NOTES

Yield – Serves 6

A LITTLE TIP

If you do not care for goat cheese, fresh mozzarella is a great substitute!

NOTES

_____

_____

_____

_____

_____

_____

_____

_____

Soups & Side Dishes

DELECTABLE DISHES THAT WILL MAKE A LASTING IMPRESSION

Butternut Squash Soup

ROBUST FLAVOR AND A SMOOTH TEXTURE RESULTS IN A WONDERFULLY SATISFYING SOUP

DIRECTIONS

Pre-heat the oven to 425 degrees F.

Peel and cube the butternut squash, discarding the seeds and stringy pulp, and place in a large glass bowl. Cut the carrots into similarly sized sticks, approximately ½-inch by 4 inches. Do not peel. Add to the bowl and toss all together with the olive oil, brown sugar, and season with 1 teaspoon of salt and 1½ teaspoons pepper.

Spread the diced vegetables in one layer onto two sheet pans without crowding. Place the sheet pans in the oven and bake for 1 hour. With a large spatula, flip the vegetables once half way through the baking time.

Remove from the oven and transfer to a large glass bowl, being sure to scrape the browned bits and oil into the bowl as well. Set aside.

In the meantime, heat 1½ tablespoons of butter in a 12-inch sauté pan over medium heat. Once hot, add the onions and shallots. Season with 1 teaspoon of salt and 1½ teaspoons pepper. Sauté for 8 to 10 minutes, until translucent and tender. Then add the garlic and chopped parsley. Sauté for another 2 minutes.

Transfer the contents of the sauté pan into the bowl of a food processor. Add the butternut squash and carrots to the food processor as well. Pour in ½ cup of the vegetable stock and purée.

Next, in a Dutch oven or stock pot, bring 6 cups of vegetable stock to a simmer. Add the roasted butternut squash purée and whisk to blend until smooth. Add the heavy cream and stir to incorporate thoroughly. Allow to come to a simmer. Remove from the heat and serve hot.

INGREDIENTS

Butternut Squash – 1 large (2½ pounds), peeled, 1-inch cubed

Carrots – 2 large, unpeeled

Olive Oil – 2 tablespoons

Brown Sugar – $\frac{1}{8}$ cup

Butter – 1½ tablespoons

Yellow Onion – 1 large, diced

Shallot – 1 large, diced

Garlic – 6 cloves, chopped

Vegetable Stock – 6½ cups

Heavy Cream – $\frac{1}{3}$ cup

Parsley (Italian Flat Leaf) – 3 tablespoons, finely chopped

Kosher Salt – 2 teaspoon, divided

Black Pepper – 3 teaspoons, divided

PREPARATION NOTES

Bake – 1 hour

Yield – Serves 6 (as a soup course)

NOTES

_____

_____

_____

_____

_____

_____

_____

_____

Classic Vegetable Soup

MY VERSION OF MY ALL-TIME FAVORITE CHILDHOOD SOUP

DIRECTIONS

In a large stockpot heat the olive oil over medium heat.

Add the potatoes, onions, red pepper flakes, salt, and black pepper to the hot pan and sauté for 5 to 7 minutes.

Add the garlic, celery, carrots, bell peppers, corn, and green beans and continue to cook for another 5 minutes.

Next, add the tomatoes, tomato paste, peas, and vegetable stock. Bring to a boil then reduce heat and simmer for 20 minutes, stirring occasionally.

Stir in the dried pasta and fresh herbs and simmer for another 5 minutes.

Turn off the heat, cover and let rest for 5 minutes.

Serve hot.

INGREDIENTS

Yellow Onion – 1 large, ¼-inch diced

Celery – 3 stalks, ¼-inch diced

Carrots – 3 large, peeled, ¼-inch diced

Yukon Gold Potatoes – 1 large, peeled, ¼-inch diced

Orange Bell Pepper – 1, seeded, ¼-inch diced

Garlic – 5 cloves, minced

Peas – 1 cup, frozen

Green Beans – 1 cup, sliced to ½-inch lengths

Corn – 1 cup, fresh or frozen

Olive Oil – 3 tablespoons

Tomatoes – 1 (15-ounce) can, diced with juice

Pasta – ¾ cup, dried stars or alphabets pasta

Vegetable Stock – 3 quarts

Kosher Salt – 1½ teaspoons

Black Pepper – 2½ teaspoons

Tomato Paste – 1 (6-ounce) can

Red Pepper Flakes – 1/8 teaspoon

Basil – 4 tablespoons, freshly chopped

Dill – 4 tablespoons, freshly chopped

Parsley – 4 tablespoons, freshly chopped

A FRESH IDEA

I like to make big batches of my Classic Vegetable Soup in the spring and summer when I can buy fresh vegetables at my local farm stands. I then store it in the freezer for those cool autumn days or wintery nights!

PREPARATION NOTES

Yield – Serves 8 to 10

NOTES

Corn Chowder

A SUMMER STAPLE, REVAMPED SPLENDIDLY

DIRECTIONS

In a large stock pot heat the oil and butter over medium heat.

Once melted, add the onions, salt, and pepper and cook for 10 to 12 minutes until the onions are softened and translucent.

Add the corn and garlic and continue to cook for another 5 minutes.

Next, add the flour and turmeric and continue to cook for an additional 3 to 5 minutes.

Pour in the vegetable stock, add the potatoes, and corn cobs. Bring the entire mixture to a boil, then reduce to a simmer and cook for 15 to 20 minutes, uncovered.

Next, remove the corn cobs and add the half and half and cheddar cheese. Cook for an additional 5 to 7 minutes.

Season with cracked pepper and salt to taste.

Serve hot.

INGREDIENTS

Corn on the Cob – 5 large ears, cut off the cob

Potatoes (Yukon Gold) – 1½ pound, peeled, ½-inch diced

Yellow Onions – 2 large, ¼-inch diced

Garlic – 5 cloves, finely minced

Vegetable Stock – 6 cups, hot

Half and Half – 1½ cups

English Cheddar – ½ pound, grated

Olive Oil – ¼ cup

Butter – 4 tablespoons, unsalted

Kosher Salt – 1½ teaspoons

Black Pepper – 2 teaspoons

Turmeric – 1 teaspoon

Flour – $^1/_3$ cup, all-purpose

PREPARATION NOTES

Yield – Serves 6

A FRESH IDEA

I love to make this every summer to welcome the start of sweet corn season! Once the soup is finished you can keep it warm for your party by placing it in a crockpot set to the lowest temperature.

NOTES

_____

_____

_____

_____

_____

_____

_____

_____

_____

Curried Split Pea Soup

HEARTY AND DELICIOUS, THIS SOUP IS SURE TO PLEASE YOUR TASTE BUDS

DIRECTIONS

Heat the olive oil in a large heavy-bottomed pot over medium heat.

Add the onion, shallot, salt, and pepper and sauté over medium heat until translucent, or about 8 to 10 minutes.

Next, add the garlic, carrots, potatoes, and curry powder and cook for an additional 5 minutes.

Stir in ¾ pound of the dried peas and vegetable stock. Bring to a boil. Then, reduce the heat and simmer uncovered for 45 minutes, stirring occasionally.

Next, add the remaining dried peas and continue to cook for another 45 minutes. The peas should be tender but still have a little bite to them.

Off the heat add the heavy cream and stir well to incorporate evenly.

Serve hot.

INGREDIENTS

Yellow Onion – 1 large, ¼-inch diced

Shallot – 1 medium-sized, ¼-inch diced

Garlic – 6 cloves, minced

Carrots – 5 carrots, ½-inch diced

Yukon Gold Potatoes – 2 medium-sized, peeled, ½-inch diced

Vegetable Stock – 3½ quarts

Dried Split Peas – 1½ pounds, divided

Olive Oil – 3 tablespoons

Curry Powder – 2 teaspoons

Kosher Salt – 1½ teaspoons

Black Pepper – 2 teaspoons

Heavy Cream – ¼ cup

PREPARATION NOTES

Yield – Serves 6

HERE'S AN IDEA

This soup pairs perfectly with my Honey Rustic Bread (page 109) and a fresh arugula salad with a simple vinaigrette dressing.

NOTES

Matzo Ball Soup with Saffron

CURING A COLD HAS NEVER BEEN SO EASY—OR DELICIOUS

DIRECTIONS

In a small bowl, whisk together the matzo meal and baking powder. Set aside.

In a large bowl, combine 2 tablespoons of olive oil, 1/3 cup of vegetable stock, eggs, salt, pepper, rosemary, thyme, and parsley and whisk together thoroughly. Next, add the dry mixture and mix until combined. Cover with plastic wrap, pressing it to the surface of the mixture. Refrigerate for 1 hour.

Meanwhile, in a 12-inch sauté pan, heat 3 tablespoons of olive oil over medium heat. Add the onions, carrots, and shallots and cook for 8 to 10 minutes, until tender. Next, add the garlic and continue cooking for another 2 minutes. Set aside.

Bring a medium-sized pot of salted water to a boil. Cook the egg noodles for 5 minutes. Drain and set aside.

In a large stockpot, bring the 5 quarts of vegetable stock to a boil, and then reduce to a simmer. Next, retrieve the matzo meal from the refrigerator and, using a standard 1¼-inch scoop, form the matzo mixture into balls and gently drop them into the simmer broth.

Add the saffron to the stockpot and cover. Cook for 30 minutes, stirring occasionally and gently being careful not to break the matzo balls. Next, remove the matzo balls from the broth and set aside on a sheet pan.

To the broth add the pasta, sautéed vegetables, and matzo balls. Simmer for 2 to 3 minutes, just long enough to heat all the ingredients through.

Ladle the hot broth and 3 to 4 matzo balls into serving bowls, being careful not to damage the matzo balls. Garnish with a sprinkle of salt, pepper, and freshly minced parsley.

INGREDIENTS

Matzo Meal – 1 cup

Eggs – 4 extra-large

Baking Powder – 1 teaspoon

Olive Oil – 5 tablespoons, divided

Kosher Salt – 1 tablespoon

Black Pepper – 1½ teaspoons

Rosemary – 1 teaspoon, freshly minced

Thyme – 2 teaspoons, freshly minced

Parsley – ¼ cup, freshly minced

Vegetable Stock – 5 quarts, plus 1/3 cup

Saffron – 1 teaspoon

Carrots – 6 large, peeled, ¼-inch diced

Yellow Onion – 1 large, ¼-inch diced

Shallots – 1 large, ¼-inch diced

Garlic – 6 cloves, minced

Pasta (Egg Noodles) – 2 cups, uncooked

PREPARATION NOTES

Yield – Serves 6

A LITTLE STORY

I lived on the Upper West Side of New York for years and that is where I had my first bowl of matzo ball soup! It quickly became my favorite meal of the autumn and winter seasons. After many versions and years of testing, Matzo Ball Soup with Saffron is now perfected! The depth of flavor in both the broth and matzo balls will be sure to warm your heart, just like it does Ryan's!

NOTES

_____

_____

_____

_____

_____

_____

_____

_____

Roasted Tomato Bisque

WITH SUCH DEPTH OF FLAVOR AND CREAMINESS THIS SOUP IS MORE LIKE BISQUE

DIRECTIONS

Pre-heat the oven to 450 degrees F.

Cut the tomatoes in half length-wise. Remove the pith and seeds. Place in a large glass bowl and toss with the olive oil and season with 1 teaspoon of salt and 1½ teaspoons black pepper.

On a sheet pan place the tomato halves skin-side up, without crowding. Use two sheet pans if necessary. Sprinkle with the sugar. Place the sheet pan(s) in the oven and bake for 1 hour.

Remove from the oven and transfer to a large glass bowl, being sure to scrape the browned bits and oil into the bowl as well. Set aside.

In the meantime, heat 1½ tablespoons of butter in a 12-inch sauté pan over medium heat. Once hot, add the onions and shallots. Season with 1 teaspoon of salt, 1½ teaspoons black pepper, and the crushed red pepper flakes. Sauté for 8 to 10 minutes, until translucent and tender. Then add the garlic and sauté for another 2 minutes.

Transfer the contents of the sauté pan into the bowl of a food processor. Add the roasted tomatoes, sun-dried tomato paste, sun-dried tomatoes, and basil leaves to the food processor as well. Pour in ½ cup of the vegetable stock and purée.

Next, in a Dutch oven or stock pot, bring 5½ cups of vegetable stock to a simmer. Add the roasted tomato purée and whisk to blend until smooth. Add the heavy cream and stir to incorporate thoroughly. Allow to come to a simmer. Remove from the heat and serve hot.

INGREDIENTS

Roma Tomatoes – 4 pounds (15 to 20 tomatoes)

Olive Oil – 2 tablespoons

Sugar – 2 tablespoons

Butter – 1½ tablespoons

Yellow Onion – 1 large, diced

Shallot – 1 large, diced

Garlic – 6 cloves, chopped

Vegetable Stock – 6 cups, divided

Sun-Dried Tomato Paste – 2 tablespoons

Sun-Dried Tomatoes – 2 tablespoons

Heavy Cream – 1/3 cup

Basil – 1 cup, fresh leaves, chopped

Crushed Red Pepper Flakes – ½ teaspoon

Kosher Salt – 2 teaspoons, divided

Black Pepper – 3 teaspoons, divided

PREPARATION NOTES

Bake – 1 hour

Yield – Serves 6 (as a soup course)

NOTES

_____

_____

_____

_____

_____

_____

_____

_____

Brown Butter Basil Corn

IN THIS DISH THE BUTTER TAKES ON A SUBTLY NUTTY FLAVOR

DIRECTIONS

In a 12-inch sauté pan set over medium heat, melt the butter and cook until it turns golden brown, or about 7 to 9 minutes.

Add the corn, salt, and pepper and sauté for 5 to 7 minutes, stirring frequently.

Remove from the heat, add basil, and toss to combine.

Serve hot.

INGREDIENTS

Corn – 2 pound, sweet corn kernels

Basil – 1 cup, freshly chopped

Butter – 6 tablespoons, unsalted, room temperature

Kosher Salt – 1 tablespoon

Black Pepper – 1 tablespoon

PREPARATION NOTES

Yield – Serves 4 to 6

ANOTHER IDEA

If fresh corn is not in season you can make Brown Butter Basil Corn with frozen corn. Defrost the corn in warm water for 5 minutes and dry thoroughly before adding to the pan.

NOTES

_____

_____

_____

_____

_____

_____

_____

_____

_____

Corn Muffins

REGARDLESS OF THE MEAL OR TIME OF DAY THESE MUFFINS ARE A PERFECT ADDITION

DIRECTIONS

Preheat oven to 400 degrees F. Butter and flour a standard 12-well muffin pan, including the top surface.

In a large bowl sift together the flour and cornmeal.

In a separate bowl, combine the eggs, milk, butter, corn, scallions, salt, pepper, and cheddar. Mix until well combined. Pour the wet mixture over the dry ingredients and stir until just combined. The batter will be lumpy.

Using a standard 2¼-inch scoop, fill the muffin wells evenly.

Bake for 20 to 25 minutes, or until lightly golden brown.

Allow the muffins to cool for 5 minutes in the muffin pan before serving.

Serve hot or at room temperature.

INGREDIENTS

Flour (self-rising) – 2½ cups

Cornmeal – ½ cup

Milk – 1 cup

Butter – 1 stick, unsalted, melted

Eggs – 2 extra-large, lightly beaten

Sweet Corn – 5 ounces canned sweet corn, drained

Scallions – 2 scallions, finely chopped

English Cheddar – 3 ounces, finely grated

Kosher Salt – ¾ teaspoon

Black Pepper – ½ teaspoon

PREPARATION NOTES

Bake – 20 to 25 minutes

Yield – Makes 12

A SIMPLE TRICK

Make these Corn Muffins ahead of time! They can be stored in an airtight container for two days prior to serving. Place them directly onto the oven rack in a preheated 350 degree F oven for 5 minutes to reheat!

NOTES

Creamy Mashed Potatoes

THE PERFECT RECIPE FOR SUNDAY DINNERS AND HOLIDAYS

DIRECTIONS

In a small skillet heat the olive oil over low heat. Cook the rosemary, thyme, and garlic for 5 to 6 minutes and set aside.

Meanwhile, in a large stock pot, boil the potatoes in well-salted water for 15 minutes or until tender. Drain and set aside.

Place a food mill fitted with a small disc-blade over a large glass bowl. Process the potatoes and olive oil mixture through the food mill, rotating the handle forward and backward to force the potatoes through the disc.

As soon as the potatoes are milled, slowly whisk in the hot milk, butter, cream cheese, salt, and pepper.

Serve hot.

INGREDIENTS

Yukon Gold Potatoes – 4 pounds, peeled, cut into quarters

Olive Oil – ¼ cup

Garlic – 8 cloves, peeled and slightly smashed

Rosemary – 1 tablespoon, freshly minced

Thyme – 2 teaspoons, freshly minced

Cream Cheese – 16 ounces, room temperature

Milk – 1 cup, heated

Kosher Salt – 1 tablespoon

Black Pepper – 1 tablespoon

Butter – 3 tablespoons, unsalted

PREPARATION NOTES

Yield – Serves 6

GIVE THIS A TRY

Mashed potatoes may be kept warm in a heat-proof bowl set over simmering water. Just cover the bowl tightly with plastic wrap first, making sure to keep it away from the flame.

NOTES

Focaccia Bread

A GREAT SAVORY BREAD TO BE SERVED WITH A "SAUCY" DISH

DIRECTIONS

In a large bowl combine the water, sugar, and yeast. Allow to fully dissolve, about 5 minutes.

Add 4 tablespoons of olive oil, flour, salt, pepper, 1 tablespoon each of rosemary and thyme, and half of the minced garlic. Stir until well combined. Turn the dough out onto a lightly floured surface and knead until dough is smooth, or about 5 minutes.

Form the dough into a ball and place in a large bowl that has been brushed with olive oil. Brush the top of the dough with a bit more olive oil. Cover with a clean towel and allow to rest in a warm place until doubled in size, about 2 hours.

Meanwhile, in a small sauté pan, over low-medium heat, add the olive oil. Then, add the remaining garlic, thyme, and rosemary. Sauté until the garlic is cooked, about 2 to 3 minutes. Be careful not to brown or burn the garlic. Remove from the heat and set aside.

Preheat the oven to 425 degrees F. Dust a sheet pan with cornmeal.

With your fist punch down the dough in the center allowing the gases to escape. Let rest for another 5 minutes.

Turn out the dough onto a lightly floured surface and roll out to fit the baking sheet (it does not have to be perfect).

Transfer the dough onto the prepared baking sheet and brush evenly with the herb and olive oil mixture.

Bake for 15 to 17 minutes, or until the top is golden brown.

Allow to cool for 10 minutes before serving.

INGREDIENTS

Water – 1 cup, warm

Yeast – ¼ ounce

Flour – 2½ cups

Olive Oil – 6 tablespoons, divided

Sugar – 2 teaspoons

Rosemary – 2 tablespoons, freshly minced, divided

Kosher Salt – ¾ teaspoon

Black Pepper – 1 teaspoon

Garlic – 6 cloves, finely minced, divided

Thyme – 2 tablespoons, freshly minced, divided

Cornmeal – $1/3$ cup

PREPARATION NOTES

Bake – 15 to 17 minutes

Yield – Serves 6 to 8

A TASTY IDEA

Try spreading 1 cup of the Spicy Oregano Sauce (page 131) on top, leaving a ¼-inch border. Sprinkle with ¾ cup of mozzarella cheese, put it under the broiler until the cheese is just melted, and serve! Instant focaccia pizza!

NOTES

_____

_____

_____

_____

_____

_____

_____

_____

_____

Fries in a Paper Bag

THESE HOME-MADE FRIES ARE WORTH THE GREASY FINGERS!

DIRECTIONS

Begin by slicing the peeled potatoes into ¼-inch wide sticks, allowing the length to be determined by the potato itself.

Fill a large bowl with ice water and soak the potatoes for at least 2 hours in the refrigerator, changing the water once during the soaking process. This can be done overnight as well.

Drain the potatoes and pat them dry very thoroughly using clean kitchen towels. Allow the potatoes to sit on a clean dry towel while preparing the oil.

Preheat the oven to 250 degrees F.

In a large stockpot, over high heat, empty the entire can of vegetable shortening into the pot. Using a candy thermometer, bring the oil to 375 degrees F.

In small batches, place the potato slices in the hot oil and fry until they are golden brown, about 7 to 10 minutes. With a slotted metal spoon, scoop out the fries and place them in a large brown paper bag. Sprinkle with desired amount of table salt and shake vigorously. Transfer the salted fries onto a baking sheet and place into the oven to keep warm. Follow the same steps until all the potatoes have been fried.

To serve, roll down the top of a new brown paper bag and transfer all the fries into the bag. Enjoy!

INGREDIENTS

Vegetable Shortening – 48 ounces

Russet Potatoes – 12 medium-sized

Table Salt – To taste

PREPARATION NOTES

Yield – Serves 4 to 6

HERE'S A TIP

The oil actual gets better with use when used just to fry potatoes. To store the oil allow it to cool partially for 30 minutes (when it is cool to handle, but still liquid). Carefully strain it through a fine mesh sieve back into the original can. Allow to cool completely before putting on the lid. Store in a cool dry pantry.

It was a family tradition to use this oil over and over again when making fries. The oil will deepen in color and flavor with each use.

A LITTLE STORY

Growing up, my Nan had a small kitchen but it was always filled with her children, grandchildren, and friends. When she wasn't playing cards and having a glass of white zinfandel, she was cooking fabulous family recipes. The entire family loved it when she made fries. Everybody would help cut the potatoes, dry them in kitchen towels, and fry them. The most fun was shaking the big brown grocery bag! Most of the time the fries never made it to the table. The big brown bag would be passed around and emptied by happy hungry fingers. Nan would make pounds of her perfectly fried potatoes! I still make these, almost once a month, repeating the exact same steps my sweet Nan did, except with a glass of merlot and Ryan shaking the big brown bag!

NOTES

_____

_____

_____

_____

_____

_____

_____

_____

Herbed Fingerling Potatoes

TENDER AND ENHANCED WITH JUST THE RIGHT HERBS

DIRECTIONS

Begin by melting the butter in a large heavy-bottomed pot (with a lid) over low heat.

Add the whole potatoes, salt, and pepper, and toss to coat. Cover the pot and let steam over low heat for 30 to 35 minutes.

During the cooking process, shake the pot, leaving the cover on, every 5 minutes to ensure the potatoes do not stick to the bottom of the pot.

Remove from the heat, leaving the cover on, and continue to steam for another 5 minutes.

Toss with dill, lemon zest, and parsley.

Serve hot either in the pot, or in a serving bowl.

INGREDIENTS

Fingerling Potatoes – 1½ pounds, rinsed

Butter – 4 tablespoons, unsalted

Kosher Salt – 1 teaspoon

Black Pepper – 1 teaspoon

Lemon Zest – ½ teaspoon, freshly zested

Parsley – 1½ teaspoons, freshly chopped

Dill – 1½ teaspoons, freshly chopped

PREPARATION NOTES

Bake – 30 to 35 minutes

Yield – Serves 4 to 6

FOOD FOR THOUGHT

Fresh dill and parsley give this side dish an elevated and well-rounded flavor. You can also substitute thyme and basil.

NOTES

_____

_____

_____

_____

_____

_____

_____

_____

_____

_____

Honey Rustic Bread

THIS BREAD IS PERFECT FOR SANDWICHES AND TARTINES

DIRECTIONS

First Day

In a large bowl, combine the water, yeast, and honey. Allow the yeast to fully dissolve, about 5 minutes.

Add flour and salt, and then stir until blended. The dough will be very sticky. Cover the bowl with plastic wrap. Let the dough rest at room temperature for 12 to 18 hours.

Next Day

Using just enough flour to keep the dough from sticking to the work surface or your fingers, quickly fold the dough over onto itself twice then shape the dough into a ball.

Lay a clean kitchen towel (not terry cloth), generously coated with flour, in a large bowl. Place the dough, seam side down, on the towel and dust with more flour. Cover the bowl with another clean kitchen towel and let rise until the dough is more than double in size, about 2 hours.

Next, preheat the oven to 450 degrees F. Place a cast iron pot with lid in the preheated oven for at least 30 minutes while the dough is rising. The pot should be at least 2¾ quart sized.

Carefully remove the pot from the oven and rest on a heat-resistant surface. To prepare the dough, remove the top cotton towel and then slide your hand under the towel laying in the bowl and turn the dough over, seam side up, into the hot cast iron pot. With potholders carefully shake the pot once or twice to evenly distribute the dough (it will even out as it bakes).

Cover the pot with the lid and bake for 30 minutes. Then, uncover and continue baking until the loaf is crusty and browned (about 15 to 20 minutes more). Keep your eye on the bread at this point as it can burn easily.

Finally, remove the pan from the oven and place the loaf on a wire rack to cool completely.

INGREDIENTS

Flour – 3 cups, all-purpose

Yeast – 1 packet, active dry yeast (¼ ounce)

Kosher Salt – 1¾ teaspoons

Honey – 4 tablespoons

Water – 1½ cups, warm

PREPARATION NOTES

Prep – Requires an over-night rise

Bake – 45 to 50 minutes

Yield – 1 loaf

NOTES

_____

_____

_____

_____

_____

_____

_____

_____

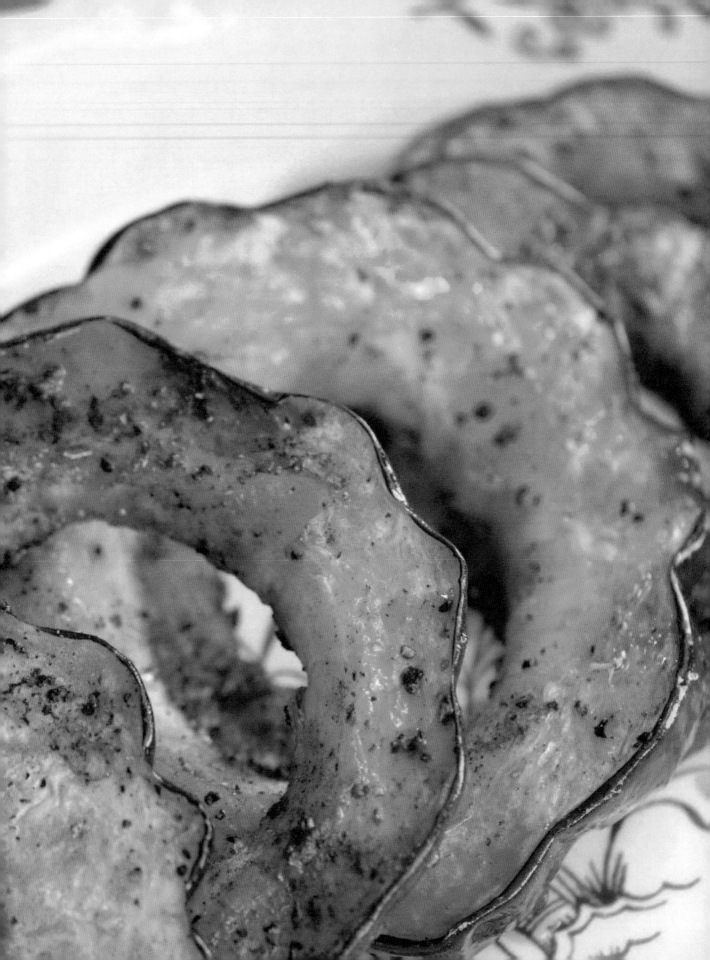

Roasted Acorn Squash

SOMETIMES IT JUST CANNOT GET ANY SIMPLER AND MORE FLAVORFUL

DIRECTIONS

Preheat oven to 400 degrees F.

Start by slicing the acorn squash into ½-inch thick slices, leaving the skin on. Next, using a small paring knife, remove the stringy center and seeds from the middle of each slice.

Place all the squash slices directly onto a sheet pan and toss with olive oil, salt, pepper, brown sugar, and cinnamon.

Ensure all the slices are lying flat on the sheet pan (it is fine if the skins touch). Roast for 40 to 45 minutes. Halfway through the baking time flip each slice once to brown evenly on both sides.

Remove the sheet pan from the oven and carefully arrange the roasted acorn squash on a serving platter. Drizzle with maple syrup and serve.

INGREDIENTS

Acorn Squash – 1 medium-sized, cut ½-inch thick, skin on

Olive Oil – 3 tablespoons

Kosher Salt – ¾ teaspoon

Black Pepper – 1 teaspoon

Brown Sugar – 1 tablespoon

Cinnamon – ½ teaspoon

Maple Syrup – 2 tablespoons

PREPARATION NOTES

Bake – 40 to 45 minutes

Yield – Serves 5 to 6 people

HERE'S A THOUGHT

Delicious with a salad for lunch or as part of a dinner feast, Roasted Acorn Squash is the perfect side for any occasion.

NOTES

_____

_____

_____

_____

_____

_____

_____

_____

_____

Roasted Vegetables

THIS SIMPLE RECIPE WILL MAKE YOUR HOUSE SMELL LIKE A HEAVENLY GARDEN

DIRECTIONS

Preheat oven to 425 degrees F.

In a large bowl combine all the ingredients, except the garlic.

Toss together to coat all the vegetables and divide evenly onto 2 half-sheet pans.

Place in the oven and roast for 20 minutes and then toss once. Sprinkle half the minced garlic onto the vegetables on each half-sheet pan.

Return to the oven and roast for an additional 20 to 30 minutes. The vegetables should be tender, but not soggy. Test with a fork, looking for a bit of resistance.

Remove the pans from the oven. Arrange the vegetables on a serving platter and garnish with a light sprinkling of salt and black pepper. Serve warm.

INGREDIENTS

Red Bell Peppers – 2 large, seeded, ½-inch diced

Carrots – 3, peeled, ½-inch diced

Red Onions – 1 large, ½-inch diced

Yellow Onions – 1 large, ½-inch diced

Butternut Squash – 2 cups, peeled, ½-inch diced

Garlic – 4 cloves, minced, divided

Kosher Salt – 1 tablespoon

Black Pepper – 1 tablespoon

Olive Oil – $^1/_3$ cup

Crushed Red Pepper Flakes – ¼ teaspoon

Thyme – 1 tablespoon, freshly minced

Rosemary – 1 tablespoon, freshly minced

PREPARATION NOTES

Bake – 40 to 50 minutes

Yield – Serves 8

A TASTY IDEA

Roasted Vegetables is the perfect way to prepare vegetables for a casual weekday meal or a fancy soirée! Use the roasted vegetables as a side dish and in the Panini with Roasted Vegetables (page 147)! They are also great left over in a simple cream sauce tossed with pasta!

NOTES

Simple Peas with Pecorino

AN EASY RECIPE FOR CASUAL ENTERTAINING

DIRECTIONS

Bring a pot of water to a boil. Cook the peas for 2 to 3 minutes, making sure they still have an al dente bite. Drain well.

In a large bowl, combine the peas, butter, salt, and pepper. Toss to coat evenly.

Using a vegetable peeler, shave big shards of Pecorino Romano onto the peas. Serve immediately.

INGREDIENTS

Petite Frozen Peas – 2 bags, 14 to 16 ounces each

Pecorino Romano – 4 ounces

Kosher Salt – 1 teaspoon

Black Pepper – 1 teaspoon

Butter – 2 teaspoons

PREPARATION NOTES

Yield – Serves 6

A LITTLE TIP

When fresh peas are in season this is a perfect way to prepare them! Blanching them sets their bright green color and allows them to retain their fresh flavor!

NOTES

_____

_____

_____

_____

_____

_____

_____

_____

Sliced Baked Potato

PERFECT TO PAIR WITH EGGS FOR BRUNCH OR A FILET MIGNON AT DINNER

DIRECTIONS

Preheat oven to 425 degrees F.

Start by slicing the bottom off the long side of each potato, and the root-end of each onion, so that each has a flat surface to stand upon.

Cut each potato and onion into ⅛-inch slices without cutting all the way through the body, leaving it connected at the base.

Arrange potatoes and onions onto a sheet pan, flat side down. Set aside.

In a small bowl, combine the butter, olive oil, garlic, salt, pepper, honey, and half of the thyme and rosemary, mixing thoroughly.

Spread 1 teaspoon of the butter mixture onto the tops of the potatoes and onions, making sure to evenly distribute the mixture and working it in-between the slices.

Bake for 40 to 45 minutes until the tops are nicely browned.

Remove from the oven, arrange on a serving platter and sprinkle with remaining rosemary and thyme.

INGREDIENTS

Potatoes – 6 medium-sized, Yukon Gold

Yellow Onions – 6 small

Garlic – 5 cloves, finely minced

Butter – 4 tablespoons, unsalted, room temperature

Olive Oil – 2 tablespoons

Kosher Salt – ¾ teaspoon

Black Pepper – ¾ teaspoon

Honey – 1 teaspoon

Thyme – 1 tablespoon, freshly minced, divided

Rosemary – 1 tablespoon, freshly minced, divided

PREPARATION NOTES

Bake – 40 to 45 minutes

Yield – Serves 6 people

A HELPFUL TIP

When slicing the potatoes and onions into 1/8-inch slices, place each potato and onion in the curved well of a large wooden (to avoid dulling your knife) spoon so that the edges of the spoon will prevent you from completely slicing through to the bottom.

NOTES

_____

_____

_____

_____

_____

_____

_____

_____

Southwest Oven Corn

LESS WORK THAN GRILLING AND PACKED WITH A REAL KICK

DIRECTIONS

Preheat oven to 425 degrees F.

In the bowl of an electric mixer fitted with a paddle attachment, combine the butter, lime juice, lime zest, cilantro, garlic, and spices. Mix on low speed until just combined.

Rub each ear of corn with 1 tablespoon of the herbed butter then tightly wrap in aluminum foil, making sure to twist the edges well to seal.

Place the wrapped ears of corn directly on the oven rack, with the seam side facing up. Place a large piece of foil on the rack below to catch any liquid from the packages.

Roast the corn for 20 to 25 minutes, depending on the size of the ears.

Carefully remove from the oven and serve hot.

INGREDIENTS

Corn – 8 ears, fresh, husked

Butter – 1 stick, unsalted, room temperature

Garlic – 8 cloves, finely minced

Lime Zest – 1 lime, freshly zested

Lime Juice – 1 tablespoon, freshly squeezed

Kosher Salt – 1 tablespoon

Black Pepper – 1 tablespoon

Hot Paprika – 2 teaspoons

Chili Powder – 1 teaspoon

Cumin – 1½ teaspoon

Crushed Red Pepper Flakes – ¼ teaspoon

Cilantro – 2 tablespoons, freshly chopped

PREPARATION NOTES

Bake – 20 to 25 minutes

Yield – Serves 8

ANOTHER IDEA

You can also make Southwest Oven corn on the grill! Simply grill 10 to 15 minutes, turning every 2 to 3 minutes.

NOTES

_____

_____

_____

_____

_____

_____

_____

_____

Main Courses

THE MAIN EVENT FOR A FABULOUS LUNCH OR INDULGENT DINNER

Apples & Sage Creamy Lasagna

THE DELICATE SAGE FLAVOR ENHANCES THE APPLES AND GRUYERE

DIRECTIONS

Preheat oven to 375 degrees F. Butter a 9 x 13 x 2-inch baking dish.

In a large sauté pan heat 4 tablespoons of butter and 2 tablespoons of olive oil over medium heat. Cook the onions for 5 to 7 minutes or until tender. Add the garlic, apples, and sage. Continue to cook for another 2 to 3 minutes. Remove from the heat and set aside.

In a small sauce pan bring the milk to a simmer and then set aside.

In a large sauce pan melt 8 tablespoons (1 stick) of butter over low heat. Add the flour and continue to cook for another 1 to 2 minutes, stirring constantly with a wooden spoon.

Pour the hot milk over the butter mixture. Add the salt, pepper, and nutmeg. Continue to cook for another 5 to 6 minutes, stirring constantly with a whisk.

To assemble the lasagna, coat the bottom of the baking dish moderately with white sauce. Arrange a layer of noodles to cover the bottom of the dish. Add $^1/_3$ of the sauce, $^1/_3$ of the apple mixture, and ¼ of both cheeses. Repeat the process twice more. Top with a final layer of noodles and sauce, and sprinkle with the remaining cheeses. You will have a total of four layers of noodles with three layers apples and cheese in-between.

Bake for 45 minutes, or until the top is browned and the sauce is bubbly and hot.

Allow to cool for 10 minutes and serve hot.

INGREDIENTS

Apples (Gala) – 5, peeled, cored, ½-inch diced

Yellow Onions – 2 large, ½-inch diced

Garlic – 4 cloves, minced

Milk – 4 cups, whole

Flour – ½ cup

Kosher Salt – 1 tablespoon

Black Pepper – 2 teaspoons

Nutmeg – 1½ teaspoons

Sage – 3 tablespoons, chopped

Olive Oil – 2 tablespoons

Lasagna Noodles – ¾ pound, no-cook noodles

Butter – 1½ sticks, unsalted, divided

Gruyere – 1½ cups, grated

Parmesan Cheese – 1½ cups, grated

PREPARATION NOTES

Bake – 45 minutes

Yield – Serves 6 to 8

HERE'S A THOUGHT

Because this dish is made with apples it is perfect to serve year-round. Apples & Sage Lasagna is also a great addition to a pot-luck!

NOTES

Autumnal Risotto

CREAMY, WARM, AND AROMATIC—A COMFORTING CASUAL DINNER DISH

DIRECTIONS

Start by combining both the vegetable stock and spiced cider in a medium sauce pan, and bring it to a boil, then reduce the heat to a simmer.

In a medium-sized heavy-bottomed stock pot melt the butter together with the olive oil. Sauté the onions, apples, salt, and pepper over medium heat until the onions are translucent, about 8 to 10 minutes. Stir occasionally.

Add the roasted butternut squash (follow the first part of the recipe for Butternut Squash Soup, page 85), minced garlic, rosemary, and thyme, and continue to cook for another 2 minutes, stirring occasionally.

In the meantime, warm the vegetable stock to just below a simmer for use in the next step.

Next, add the dry rice and stir until well coated and slightly translucent, or about 2 minutes. Stir in 1 cup of the hot stock mixture and simmer gently, stirring regularly.

After the stock has been mostly absorbed into the rice add another cup of stock and let simmer and absorb. Continue this same process until the rice is cooked, about 18 to 22 minutes. When taste-testing the rice it should have a bit of a "bite" to it and be slightly al dente.

Stir in the heavy cream and shredded Parmesan cheese. Remove from the heat, cover the pot, and let stand for just a few minutes before serving.

INGREDIENTS

Yellow Onions – 2 large, chopped

Apple (Gala) – 1, peeled, cored, ½-inch diced

Garlic – 3 cloves, minced

Olive Oil – 2 tablespoons

Butter – 1 tablespoon

Butternut Squash – 1½ cups, ½-inch diced, roasted (see page 85)

Kosher Salt – 2 teaspoons

Black Pepper – 1½ teaspoons, freshly cracked

Rosemary – 2 teaspoons, freshly minced

Thyme – 2 teaspoons, freshly minced

Vegetable Stock – 4 cups, hot

Arborio Rice – 2 cups (uncooked)

Spiced Apple Cider – 1 cup

Heavy Cream – ½ cup

Parmesan Cheese – 1 cup, shredded

PREPARATION NOTES

Yield – Serves 6

FOOD FOR THOUGHT

Serve with a crusty baguette and baby arugula salad. I recommend a classically-themed balsamic vinaigrette for the salad (which you could enhance with a splash of citrus, such as orange). The savory and slightly sweet risotto pairs wonderfully with a peppery bold red zinfandel. You can also serve the Autumnal Risotto as a delicious warm side dish.

A LITTLE TIP

Leftovers can be kept in the refrigerator. When re-heating, do so over a low-medium flame and add ¼ cup of either heavy cream or vegetable stock. Add a little more or less depending on the amount you are re-heating. When you have a creamy (but not wet) consistency it is ready.

NOTES

Citrus Farfalle

THIS CREAMY PASTA IS LIGHT AND BRIGHT, PERFECT FOR A SUNNY LUNCHEON

DIRECTIONS

Begin by heating a large sauté pan on medium heat and add 2 tablespoon of butter. Once hot, add the diced onion and shallot. Season with the salt and black pepper. Sauté for 10 minutes until translucent and tender. Add the garlic and lemon zest. Sauté for another 2 to 3 minutes.

Next, add the vegetable stock and lemon juice to the pan. Simmer for 5 minutes on medium-low heat, stirring occasionally. In the meantime, in a small dish combine 1 tablespoon of flour and 1 tablespoon of butter with a small fork. Then add the butter and flour mixture to the pan. Stir to fully dissolve and simmer for 2 minutes.

Add the cream and mascarpone to the mixture. Stir to fully incorporate and simmer for another 5 minutes.

In a large pot of well-salted water cook the farfalle to package instructions for al dente. Then drain and pour directly into the sauté pan. Toss the pasta and sauce together to coat. Transfer to a large serving bowl and garnish with parsley, basil, and a bit more lemon zest.

Serve hot.

INGREDIENTS

Yellow Onion – 1 large, ¼-inch diced

Shallot – 1 large, ¼-inch diced

Garlic – 10 cloves, minced

Butter – 3 tablespoons, unsalted, divided

Flour – 1 tablespoon

Lemon Zest – 3 tablespoons, freshly zested

Lemon Juice – ½ of a small lemon

Vegetable Stock – ²/₃ cup

Heavy Cream – ½ cup

Mascarpone – ¼ cup

Salt – 1 teaspoon

Black Pepper – 2 teaspoons, freshly cracked

Farfalle – 1 pound (dry)

Parsley (Italian Flat Leaf) – For garnish, finely chopped

Basil – For garnish, fresh leaves, finely chopped

PREPARATION NOTES

Yield – Serves 4

HERE'S AN IDEA

To add a bit of heat, add ¼ teaspoon of crushed red pepper flakes while sautéing the onions!

NOTES

Crispy Eggplant Parmesan

QUITE SIMPLY AN INSTANT FAVORITE EVERY TIME

DIRECTIONS

Preheat oven to 200 degrees F.

Start by combining the milk and eggs in a large shallow plate or dish.

In a separate large shallow plate or dish, combine the bread crumbs, ½ cup of Parmesan cheese, flour, dried basil, red pepper flakes, salt, and black pepper.

Using a paper towel, pat each slice of eggplant dry. Next, dip each side of the eggplant into the bread crumb mixture, then the egg, and finishing with the bread crumbs again. Repeat the process until all slices have been prepared. Set aside.

In a 12-inch sauté pan heat both oils and butter over medium-high heat. Fry the eggplant for 4 to 5 minutes on each side, or until golden brown and crispy. Remove the eggplant and place on a baking sheet. Transfer to the oven to keep warm.

Continue the same process until all the eggplant slices have been fried. With a slotted spoon, remove any crumbs that accumulate in the pan over the course of the frying process.

Arrange the eggplant on a serving platter, top with Spicy Oregano Sauce (page 131) and a generous portion of Parmesan cheese, freshly grated or shaved.

INGREDIENTS

Eggs – 3 extra-large, slightly beaten

Bread Crumbs (plain) – 2 cups

Kosher Salt – ¾ teaspoon

Black Pepper – 2 teaspoons

Basil (dried) – 2 teaspoons

Flour – 3 tablespoons, all-purpose

Crushed Red Pepper Flakes – $\frac{1}{8}$ teaspoon

Eggplant – 1 large, peeled, ¼-inch sliced

Olive Oil – ½ cup

Vegetable Oil – ½ cup

Butter – 2 tablespoons, unsalted

Milk – 2 tablespoons

Parmesan Cheese – 1½ cups, freshly grated, divided

PREPARATION NOTES

Yield – Serves 4

A LITTLE STORY

I will never forget the first time I made this for Ryan. He had mentioned more than once how much he did not care for eggplant. One evening he arrived home from the office and walked into the kitchen to find me with a glass of wine, candles lit, my favorite Italian music (songs my dad and great grandmother used to sing) belting from the speakers, and the mouthwatering smell of fried eggplant slices crisping away in the pan! Without missing a beat Ryan topped off my glass, poured one for him, turned up the music, and joined me in the breading process! We danced around the kitchen singing, drinking, and laughing. Once we sat down and he took his first bite he was hooked. Now, it is quite often his first request any time I ask what we should have for dinner.

NOTES

_____

_____

_____

_____

_____

_____

_____

_____

Spicy Oregano Sauce

MAMA MIA! THIS SAUCE HAS A KICK THAT WILL GIVE ANY DISH A FANTASTIC ZING

DIRECTIONS

Heat the olive oil and butter in a large heavy-bottomed pot.

Add the onions, salt, black pepper, and red pepper flakes to the hot pan and sauté over medium heat until translucent or about 8 to 10 minutes.

Add the oregano by rubbing it between the palms of your hands directly into the pot. This method helps to release the natural oils from the dried herb and will enhance the flavor of your sauce.

Next, add the garlic and honey and cook for an additional 1 to 2 minutes.

Stir in the tomatoes and simmer uncovered on low heat for 1 hour, stirring occasionally.

Presto!

INGREDIENTS

Yellow Onion – 1 large, ¼-inch diced

Garlic – 6 cloves, minced

Dried Oregano – 2 tablespoons

Crushed Red Pepper Flakes – ¾ teaspoon

Black Pepper – 2 teaspoons

Kosher Salt – 2 teaspoons

Olive Oil – 3 tablespoons

Butter – 2 tablespoons, unsalted

San Marzano Tomatoes – 3 (28-ounce) cans, crushed

Honey – 2 tablespoons

PREPARATION NOTES

Yield – Makes 6 cups

A TASTY IDEA

Serve this sauce with my Crispy Eggplant Parmesan (page 129), or with your favorite pasta cooked al dente!

NOTES

_____

_____

_____

_____

_____

_____

_____

_____

Enchilada Vegetal

¡ESTA COMIDA VEGETARIANA ES MUY DELICIOSA!

DIRECTIONS

Pre-heat oven to 350 degrees.

In a Dutch oven or stock pot, over medium-high heat, melt the butter. Once hot, add the diced onions, red bell pepper, and corn. Sauté for 5 minutes. Season with the salt, black pepper, and crushed red pepper flakes. Then, add the garlic and jalapeños. Continue to sauté for another 2 minutes.

Next, reduce the heat to medium and add the cans of fire roasted tomatoes, enchilada sauce, black beans, and green chilies. Bring to a simmer and then add the cayenne pepper and hot paprika. Cook for 10 minutes, stirring occasionally.

Remove from the heat and let cool for a few minutes. Meanwhile, in a medium-sized bowl, blend the three shredded cheeses.

In two 9 x 13-inch casserole dishes, spoon enough sauce to lightly coat the bottom of each dish. Next, place a tortilla in the sauce to coat lightly on both sides. Lay the tortilla in a casserole dish, sprinkle ¼ cup of the blended cheese mixture down the center, and spoon enough enchilada sauce into the center of the tortilla that when rolled closed it is 2 inches in diameter. Align the first completed tortilla to one end of the dish. Repeat the process to fill each casserole dish with 8 filled tortillas.

Spoon a generous portion of sauce over each full dish of enchiladas and then evenly sprinkle the remaining cheese over each full casserole dish.

Place in the oven and bake for 50 minutes, until the cheese is bubbly and browned. Remove from the oven and let rest for 10 minutes.

Garnish with fresh cilantro. Serve directly from the casserole dishes.

A TASTY IDEA

Serve Enchiladas Vegetal alongside the Green Pea Guacamole (page 59) and with the Front Porch Lemonade (page 203) for a delicious summer dinner.

PREPARATION NOTES

Bake – 50 minutes

Yield – Serves 6 to 8

INGREDIENTS

Fire Roasted Tomatoes – 2 (28-ounce) cans, diced or crushed

Green Chilies – 2 (4½-ounce) cans

Enchilada Sauce – 2 (15-ounce) cans

Red Bell Pepper – 2 large, ¼-inch diced

Yellow Onion – 2 large, ¼-inch diced

Red Onion – 1 large, ¼-inch diced

Black Beans – 2 (15-ounce) can, drained

Jalapeños – 2 tablespoons, pickled, seeded, diced

Garlic – 8 cloves, minced

Corn – 2 (15-ounce can), well drained

Cilantro – ½ cup, fresh, chopped

Kosher Salt – 3 teaspoons

Black Pepper – 3 teaspoons

Flour Tortillas – 16

Butter – 4 tablespoons, unsalted

Crushed Red Pepper Flakes – 2 teaspoon

Cayenne Pepper – 1 teaspoon

Hot Paprika – 2 teaspoons

Pepper Jack Cheese – 1 pound, shredded

Mozzarella – 1 pound, shredded

Cheddar Cheese – 1 pound, shredded

Sour Cream – For garnish

NOTES

Filet de Bœuf au Poivre

CLASSIC FRENCH BISTRO GOURMET—A FILET MIGNON IN AMERICA

DIRECTIONS

Remove the filet(s) from the refrigerator and unwrap. Let rest at room temperature for 30 minutes.

In a small shallow dish pour the salt and cracked black pepper and combine. Pat the filets dry with a paper towel.

Next, heat a cast iron skillet to high heat.

Dip the filet in the salt and black pepper mixture to coat all sides. Do not press the filet.

Place a ½ teaspoon pad of butter in the hot skillet and immediately place the filet on the pad. Place the remaining ½ teaspoon pad of butter on the top of the steak.

Pan-fry the filet for 5 to 6 minutes. Then flip and continue to cook for another 5 minutes. This cooking time will result in a medium doneness.

Remove from the heat. Transfer to a plate, pour the juices from the skillet over the steak, and cover with aluminum foil. Allow to rest for 5 minutes.

Plate and serve immediately.

INGREDIENTS

Filet Mignon (Grass-Fed) – 9-ounce steak

Coarse Salt – 1 tablespoon

Black Pepper – 1 tablespoon, freshly cracked

Butter – 1 teaspoon

PREPARATION NOTES

Yield – 1 serving (simply multiply per guest)

A LITTLE STORY

Sometimes it is the simplest meals that can be the most satisfying. Each year for Ryan's birthday I cook a Filet de Bœuf au Poivre and serve with a Caesar Salad with Hearts of Romaine (page 79), Creamy Mashed Potatoes (page 101), and a cabernet sauvignon. I think he looks forward to his birthday dinner more than he does his presents!

NOTES

Grilled Gruyere

AN ELEGANT AND SAVORY GRILLED CHEESE THAT IS STILL JUST AS SIMPLE TO PREPARE

DIRECTIONS

In a 12-inch sauté pan heat the olive oil over medium-low heat.

Once the oil is hot, add onions, salt, and pepper and cook for 5 minutes, stirring occasionally.

Add the sugar and balsamic vinegar and continue cooking for another 15 minutes.

Next, add the garlic and cook 1 to 2 minutes more, being careful not to burn the garlic. Remove from heat and set aside.

Spread ½ tablespoon of butter on one side of each piece of bread.

Assemble each sandwich by placing a slice of bread, 4 ounces of Gruyere, ¼ of the onion mixture, 5 basil leaves and then another slice of bread. Repeat the same process for the other 3 sandwiches. Make sure you keep the buttered side of each slice facing outwards.

Heat a large skillet or griddle over low-medium heat and cook each sandwich for 5 to 6 minutes on each side, until an even golden brown.

INGREDIENTS

Yellow Onion – 1 large, ¼-inch sliced

Gruyere Cheese – 16 ounces, sliced $^1/_8$-inch thick

Olive Oil – 3 tablespoons

Kosher Salt – ½ teaspoon

Black Pepper – ½ teaspoon

Basil – 20 fresh basil leaves

Bread – 8 slices, Honey Rustic Bread

Butter – 4 tablespoons, unsalted, room temperature, divided

Sugar – 1 teaspoon

Garlic – 2 cloves, finely minced

Balsamic Vinegar – 3 tablespoons

PREPARATION NOTES

Yield – Serves 4

HERE'S AN IDEA

Cut each sandwich into smaller pieces and serve with a glass of wine during movie night at home. Fancy finger food at its finest!

NOTES

I Get a Kick Out of You Chili

HIT 'EM WHERE IT COUNTS—IN THE TASTE BUDS

DIRECTIONS

In a Dutch oven or stock pot, over medium-high heat, melt the butter. Once hot, add the diced onions and sauté for 3 minutes. Season with ½ teaspoon of salt, 1 teaspoon of black pepper, and crushed red pepper flakes. Then, add the bell peppers and continue to sauté for another 5 minutes. Next, add the garlic and sauté for 2 minutes.

Add the beef grounds and stir to combine. Reduce the heat to medium-low. Cook for 5 minutes.

In a small glass bowl combine all of the remaining spices: Chili Powder, Cumin, Cayenne Pepper, Hot Paprika, 1 teaspoon of salt, and 2 teaspoons of black pepper.

Thoroughly drain the black beans and add to the onions and peppers. Add the can of crushed fire-roasted tomatoes. Stir all together. Bring to a gentle simmer, and then reduce the heat to low.

Add the combined spices and the tomato paste. Stir to mix thoroughly.

Place the lid on the Dutch oven and reduce the heat to simmer/low. At this point you can transfer the contents to a slow cooker and set to low heat. On the stove, keep covered and cook for 1 hour, stirring occasionally. In the slow cooker set to low heat cook for 3 hours.

Serve hot.

INGREDIENTS

Butter – 3 tablespoons, unsalted

Yellow Onion – 1 large, medium diced

Red Onion – 1 large, medium diced

Fire-Roasted Tomatoes – 1 (28-ounce) can, crushed

Tomato Paste – 3 ounces

Garlic – 6 cloves, minced

Black Beans – 1 (15-ounce) can

Orange Bell Pepper – 1 large, medium diced

Red Bell Pepper – 1 large, medium diced

Hot Paprika – 1½ teaspoons

Cumin – ½ teaspoon

Crushed Red Pepper – 1 teaspoon

Cayenne Pepper – ¼ teaspoon

Chili Powder – 3 tablespoons

Kosher Salt – 2 teaspoon, divided

Black Pepper – 3 teaspoon, divided

Meatless Ground Beef – 12 ounces, Quorn® Grounds recommended

PREPARATION NOTES

Yield – Serves 6

TRY THIS

Have a hearty bread on hand to help your guests get every last bite. This is a great make-in-advance dish that requires very little attention while you are entertaining. You can also make this dish with ground beef or shredded chicken.

NOTES

_____

_____

_____

_____

_____

_____

_____

_____

_____

Italian Stuffed Shells

MANGIÀ! BUON APPETITO!

DIRECTIONS

Preheat oven to 350 degrees F. Butter a 9 x 13 x 2-inch baking dish.

In a large mixing bowl combine the basil, parsley, ricotta, gorgonzola, mascarpone, 1 cup each of the mozzarella and parmesan, red pepper flakes, salt, black pepper, oregano, and nutmeg. Stir until well combined.

Cover the bottom of the baking dish with half of the sauce.

Fill the cooked shells with the cheese mixture, about 2 tablespoons per shell. Arrange the shells in the prepared dish. Spoon the remaining sauce over the filled shells and sprinkle with the remaining mozzarella and parmesan.

Bake in the lower third of the oven until the filling is heated through and the top is golden brown, about 30 minutes.

Allow to sit for 10 minutes before serving.

INGREDIENTS

Ricotta – 15 ounces, room temperature

Mascarpone – 8 ounces, room temperature

Mozzarella – 2 cups, freshly grated, divided

Parmesan Cheese – 2 cups, freshly grated, divided

Gorgonzola – $1/3$ pound, crumbled

Kosher Salt – 1 teaspoon

Black Pepper – 1 teaspoon, freshly cracked

Nutmeg – $1/8$ teaspoon

Basil – ½ cups, freshly chopped

Oregano (dried) – 1 teaspoon

Crushed Red Pepper Flakes – ½ teaspoon

Marc's Home-Style Tuscan Tomato Sauce – 3 cups, divided (page 143)

Shells – 30 large, cooked to package directions

Parsley (flat leaf) – ½ cup, freshly chopped

PREPARATION NOTES

Bake – 30 minutes

Yield – Serves 6

A LITTLE STORY

My Italian Stuffed Shells were inspired by my Godmother who makes these by the tray-full for every family gathering and holiday. My Italian Stuffed Shells might be the creamiest you have ever had! The addition of the gorgonzola gives the cheese filling a little bada-bing zing!

NOTES

_____

_____

_____

_____

_____

_____

_____

_____

Marc's Home-Style Tuscan Tomato Sauce

FROM THE OLD COUNTRY WITH A NEW GENERATION'S TWIST

DIRECTIONS

Heat the olive oil and butter in a large heavy-bottomed pot.

Add the onions, red and yellow bell peppers, salt, and black pepper to the hot pan and sauté over medium heat until translucent, or about 8 to 10 minutes.

Next, add the garlic and cinnamon and cook for an additional 1 to 2 minutes.

Stir in the tomatoes and simmer uncovered on low heat for 1 hour, stirring occasionally.

Just before serving stir in basil. Serve immediately.

INGREDIENTS

San Marzano Tomatoes – 3 (28-ounce) cans, crushed

Yellow Onion – 1 small, ¼-inch diced

Red Onion – 1 small, ¼-inch diced

Yellow Bell Pepper – 1 small, ¼-inch diced

Red Bell Pepper – 1 small, ¼-inch diced

Garlic – 6 cloves, minced

Kosher Salt – 2 teaspoons

Black Pepper – 2 teaspoons

Olive Oil – 2 tablespoons

Butter – 1 tablespoon, unsalted

Cinnamon – $\frac{1}{8}$ teaspoon

Basil – 2 cups, freshly chopped

PREPARATION NOTES

Yield – Makes 8 cups

HERE'S AN IDEA

The warmth that the hint of cinnamon brings to this sauce is perfect for the Farfalle Skewers (page 55)! Or, serve Marc's Home-Style Tuscan Tomato Sauce over steamed cabbage for a delicious (and healthy) Irish-Italian main dish!

NOTES

_____

_____

_____

_____

_____

_____

_____

_____

_____

Sautéed Gnocchi with Pancetta & Peas

THESE SIMPLE LITTLE PILLOWS OF POTATO HEAVEN ARE ALWAYS A HIT

DIRECTIONS

Begin by bringing a pot of well-salted water to a boil for the gnocchi (following the package instructions). Boil the gnocchi for 2/3 of the instructed time. When the gnocchi are ready remove from the boiling water and drain well. Set aside.

Heat a 14-inch sauté pan over medium heat and melt 4 tablespoons of butter and 2 tablespoons of olive oil. Once the pan is hot add the pancetta and cook for 4 minutes. Add the shallots and garlic and cook for another 2 minutes.

Next, add the drained gnocchi, salt, and pepper into the sauté pan and continue to cook for another 6 minutes, stirring occasionally to ensure they do not stick together.

Add the white wine to the pan and scrape up the browned bits from the bottom of the pan. Allow to reduce for two minutes.

Then, add the heavy cream and allow to return to a simmer.

Next, add the peas, bring back to a simmer, and then remove from the heat.

Lastly, add the Parmesan cheese and stir to incorporate well. Serve hot.

INGREDIENTS

Gnocchi – 1 pound, fresh

Peas – 2 cups, frozen

Pancetta – 4 ounces, small-diced

Garlic – 8 cloves, finely minced

Butter – 4 tablespoons

Olive Oil – 2 tablespoons

Shallots – 2 medium, finely diced

Kosher Salt – ½ teaspoons

Black Pepper – 1 teaspoon, freshly cracked

Parmesan Cheese – ¾ cup, freshly grated

Heavy Cream – 1 cup

White Wine – ½ cup, Sauvignon Blanc

PREPARATION NOTES

Yield – Serves 4

NOTES

Panini with Roasted Vegetables

PROBABLY THE MOST FABULOUS WAY TO EAT YOUR VEGGIES

DIRECTIONS

Spread ½ tablespoon of butter on one side of each piece of bread.

Assemble each sandwich by stacking a slice of bread (buttered side out), 2 slices of cheese, 1 cup of the roasted vegetables, 4 basil leaves, and then another slice of bread. Repeat the same process for the other 5 sandwiches.

Heat a large skillet or griddle over low-medium heat and cook each sandwich for 6 to 7 minutes on each side, until they are an even golden brown.

INGREDIENTS

Roasted Vegetables – 6 cups (page 113)

Basil – 18 leaves, fresh

Honey Rustic Bread – 12 slices (page 109)

Swiss Cheese – 12 slices

Butter – 6 tablespoons, divided

PREPARATION NOTES

Yield – 6 Panini

HERE'S AN IDEA

This is the perfect sandwich to use up left-over roasted vegetables to create a delicious and satisfying lunch! Serve it with the Caesar Salad with Hearts of Romaine (page 79) and a crisp glass of white wine.

NOTES

Pappardelle with Spinach & Sweet Italian Sausage
BOTH DELICATE AND BOLD—YOU WON'T BE ABLE TO PUT YOUR FORK DOWN

DIRECTIONS

In a large sauté pan over medium-high heat melt 1 tablespoon of butter. Crumble the sweet Italian sausage, about the size of marbles, into the pan. Cook the sausage crumbles until browned on all sides, approximately 12 minutes. With a slotted spoon, remove the browned sausage and set aside on a plate covered with a paper towel.

Next, in the same sauté pan (do not wipe it out) add the diced onion and shallot. Season with the salt and pepper. Sauté for 8 minutes, until translucent and tender. Reduce the heat to medium and add the garlic. Sauté for another 2 minutes.

Add 1 cup of vegetable stock to the pan and deglaze, scraping up any browned bits. Simmer for 5 minutes. In the meantime, in a small dish combine 1 tablespoon of flour and 1 tablespoon of butter with a small fork. Then add the butter and flour mixture to the pan. Stir to fully dissolve and simmer for 2 minutes.

Next, add the heavy cream and mascarpone to the pan. Stir to fully incorporate and simmer for another 5 minutes.

Add the spinach leaves directly to the pan. Let stand for 1 minute, and then gently fold the sauce over the leaves to coat until the spinach is wilted.

Next, add the sausage back into the pan and stir to mix.

In a large pot of well-salted water cook the Pappardelle to package instructions. Drain and immediately pour into the sauté pan. Toss the sauce and pasta together to coat. Transfer to a large serving bowl. Serve hot.

INGREDIENTS

Butter – 3 tablespoons, unsalted, room temperature, divided

Yellow Onion – 1 large, small diced

Shallot – 1 large, small diced

Garlic – 5 cloves, minced

Kosher Salt – 1 teaspoon

Black Pepper – 1½ teaspoons, freshly cracked

Flour – 1 tablespoon

Vegetable Stock – 1 cup

Mascarpone – ¼ cup

Heavy Cream – ½ cup

Baby Spinach Leaves – ⅔ pound

Sweet Italian Sausage – ½ pound, crumbled

Pappardelle – ¾ pound

PREPARATION NOTES

Yield – Serves 6

NOTES

_____

_____

_____

_____

_____

_____

_____

_____

Parsley Peppercorn & Fettuccini

SIMPLE INGREDIENTS, EASY ASSEMBLY, FABULOUS FLAVOR

DIRECTIONS

Choose your favorite Fettuccine and cook following the box instructions.

Meanwhile, in a 12-inch sauté pan heat the olive oil over low heat. Add the garlic, red pepper flakes, salt, and black pepper. Sauté for 6 minutes until the garlic is tender but not brown. Turn off the heat.

When the pasta reaches al dente reserve a ½ cup of the pasta water in a heat-proof measuring cup, then drain the pasta using a colander.

Immediately transfer the drained pasta into the sauté pan with the garlic. Add the butter and minced parsley and toss. If the pasta seems dry add back a bit of the reserved pasta water as needed and toss.

Transfer to a large serving bowl and serve hot.

INGREDIENTS

Fettuccine – ¾ pound, cooked al dente

Crushed Red Pepper Flakes – 1/8 teaspoon

Kosher Salt – ¾ teaspoon

Black Pepper – 1 teaspoon

Truffle Butter – 3 tablespoons

Olive Oil – 3 tablespoons

Parsley – 6 tablespoons, minced

Garlic – 5 cloves, minced

PREPARATION NOTES

Yield – Serves 6

HERE'S AN IDEA

This simple yet delicious pasta dish is perfect for a mid-week dinner or a Saturday night soirée! Try tossing in 1 cup of grape tomatoes that have been cut in half lengthwise.

NOTES

_____

_____

_____

_____

_____

_____

_____

_____

_____

Potato & Pecorino Pizza

THIS PIZZA WILL SURPRISE EVEN THE MOST DISCERNING PALETTES

DIRECTIONS

Preheat oven to 400 degrees F.

First, slice the potatoes, skins on, into 1/8-inch thin slices (a mandolin will work well for this task). Place the potato slices in a large bowl of ice water for 1 hour, changing the water half way through.

Remove the potatoes from the water bath, dry thoroughly with a clean kitchen towel and arrange in a single layer on a sheet pan lined with parchment paper. Bake the potato slices for 10 minutes. Remove the tray from the oven and set aside.

Lower the oven temperature to 350 degrees F.

Next, roll out the pizza pie dough into a 12-inch diameter disc, approximately ½-inch thick. Brush the dough with a light coating of olive oil.

Sprinkle ¼ cup of the cheese onto the pizza dough. Arrange the potatoes in a circular pattern, overlapping slightly and evenly covering the whole dough disc. Sprinkle with the remaining cheese, ¾ teaspoon of both the thyme and rosemary, and the salt and pepper.

Place into the oven and bake for 25 to 30 minutes, or until the outer crust is golden brown.

Remove from the oven, sprinkle with remaining rosemary and thyme.

Using a sharp pizza cutter, cut the pizza pie into the desired size pieces and serve hot.

INGREDIENTS

Pizza Dough – 16-ounce store-bought pizza pie dough

Yukon Gold Potatoes – 2 medium-sized, sliced $^1/_8$-inch thick

Olive Oil – 1 tablespoon

Pecorino Romano – 1 cup, freshly grated, divided

Rosemary – 1½ teaspoons, freshly minced, divided

Thyme – 1½ teaspoons, freshly minced, divided

Kosher Salt – ¼ teaspoon

Black Pepper – ½ teaspoon

PREPARATION NOTES

Bake – 25 to 30 minutes

Yield – 12-inch pizza pie

A LITTLE STORY

When Ryan and I lived in Seattle our South Lake Union neighborhood had a fabulous gourmet pizza restaurant. After ordering the same pizza over and over again I decided to re-create it at home, only to make it simpler by using good store-bought pizza dough. After a few tries, I got it down, perfectly! Whenever we ate there again, I was finally able to order something different from the menu!

NOTES

Pumpkin & Basil Cannelloni

A GREAT "MAKE-AHEAD" DISH FOR EASY AND ELEGANT ENTERTAINING

DIRECTIONS

Preheat oven to 350 degrees F.

Lightly butter a 9x13-inch baking dish and set aside.

In a large sauté pan, heat olive oil and butter over medium heat.

Add onions, red pepper flakes, ¾ teaspoon of salt, and ¾ teaspoon of black pepper and cook for 10 to 12 minutes, stirring occasionally. The onions should be softened and tender, but not browned.

Add garlic and balsamic vinegar and cook another 2 minutes. Remove from heat.

In the bowl of an electric mixer fitted with a paddle attachment, combine pumpkin, goat cheese, mozzarella, basil, thyme, allspice, 1 teaspoon of salt, 1 teaspoon of pepper, and brown sugar. Mix on low speed until incorporated.

Next, transfer mixture into a large pastry bag fitted with a large round tip.

Fill each cannelloni shell by standing the shell on its end, place the tip inside the top end and pipe in the mixture until the shell is filled. Repeat the process for all remaining shells.

Line the prepared baking dish with the filled cannelloni by placing each side by side, going down the full length of the pan.

Sprinkle with 1 cup of Manchego, the entire onion mixture and then the rest of the Manchego.

Cover with foil and bake for 55 minutes. Remove foil and bake for another 5 minutes, until lightly browned and bubbly.

Garnish with ½ cup fresh basil and enjoy!

HERE'S AN IDEA

If you cannot find cannelloni shells, you can also use lasagna noodles. Pre-cook the noodles according to package directions. Lay each noodle flat and pipe the pumpkin mixture down one side. Roll up the lasagna noodle and you will have a delicious alternative to cannelloni. There is no excuse not to try this warm and flavorful dish!

INGREDIENTS

Yellow Onion – 1 large, ½-inch slices

Garlic – 5 large cloves, minced

Balsamic Vinegar – 1 tablespoon

Kosher Salt – 1¾ teaspoon, divided

Black Pepper – 1¾ teaspoon, divided

Red Pepper Flakes – ¼ teaspoon

Butter – 1 tablespoon, unsalted

Olive Oil – 1 tablespoon

Pumpkin – 1 (29-ounce) can, pumpkin (not filling)

Goat Cheese – 6 ounces, room temperature

Mozzarella – ½ cup, finely shredded

Fresh Thyme – 1 tablespoon, minced

Fresh Basil – 1½ cups, roughly chopped, divided

Brown Sugar – 2 tablespoons

Allspice – ¼ teaspoon

Manchego Cheese – 2 cups, grated

Cannelloni – 28 shells, cooked to package instructions

PREPARATION NOTES

Bake – 60 minutes

Yield – Serves 6 to 8

NOTES

_____

_____

_____

_____

_____

_____

_____

_____

Rigatoni con Pomodoro e Vodka
A SOUTHERN ITALY-INSPIRED DISH WITH WONDERFULLY COMPLEX FLAVORS

DIRECTIONS

Begin by heating a large sauté pan on medium heat. Add the olive oil and 1 tablespoon of butter. Once hot, add the diced onion and shallot. Season with the salt and black pepper. Sauté for 12 to 15 minutes until translucent and tender. Add the garlic and capers. Sauté for another 2 to 3 minutes.

Next, pour the vodka into the center of the pan. If using a gas stove, do this off the heat, and then resume. Deglaze the pan, scraping up any bits from the bottom of the pan. Simmer for 8 minutes.

Add the sun-dried tomato paste and the anchovy paste. With a wooden spoon, break up and melt into the onions and vodka. Then add the crushed tomatoes, reduce the heat to low, and simmer for 10 minutes.

Next, add 2 tablespoons of butter and the heavy cream. Stir together to fully melt the butter and incorporate the cream. Simmer for another 8 minutes.

Meanwhile, bring a large pot of well-salted water to a boil and cook the rigatoni to package instructions for al dente. Then, add the well-drained pasta to the sauté pan and toss to coat thoroughly.

Transfer to a large serving bowl, sprinkle with parmesan, and serve hot.

INGREDIENTS

Olive Oil – 3 tablespoons

Butter – 3 tablespoons, divided

Yellow Onion – 1 large, diced

Shallot – 1 large, diced

Garlic – 6 cloves, chopped

Capers – 2 tablespoons, drained

Kosher Salt – 1 teaspoon

Black Pepper – 1½ teaspoons, freshly cracked

Vodka – 1 cup

Crushed Tomatoes – 1 (28-ounce) can, San Marzano

Sun-Dried Tomato Paste – 5 tablespoons

Anchovy Paste – 1 teaspoon

Heavy Cream – ½ cup

Rigatoni – ½ pound (dry)

Parmesan Cheese – ½ cup, grated or shaved

PREPARATION NOTES

Yield – Serves 6

A TASTY IDEA

Choose the biggest-diameter rigatoni you can find (or make!) for this dish. Once tossed with the vodka sauce the pasta holds delicious bites of the sauce inside. Cooked just to al dente each bite will be a little taste of southern Italian heaven.

NOTES

Roasted Butternut Squash Puttanesca

THE CREAMY TEXTURE AND LAYERS OF FLAVORS CREATE A COMFORTING HIT

DIRECTIONS

Preheat oven to 400 degrees F.

In a large bowl toss the butternut squash pieces with 3 tablespoons of olive oil and 1 teaspoon each of salt and pepper. Place the butternut squash pieces in a single layer on a sheet pan and bake for 45 minutes. Toss once halfway through the baking time.

Place a food mill fitted with a course blade over a large bowl. In small batches, purée the roasted squash. Once complete, set aside.

Begin cooking the rigatoni, following the package instructions for al dente. Reserve ¼ cup of the pasta water before draining.

Next, in a large sauté pan heat 2 tablespoons of olive oil and butter over medium heat. Sauté the onions and red bell peppers with the salt, black pepper, and sugar for about 10 minutes or until the onions and red bell peppers are tender. Add the garlic and capers, and cook for an additional 3 to 4 minutes.

Add the tomatoes, butternut squash purée, and butter. Simmer for 5 minutes. Then, add the heavy cream and simmer for another 1 to 2 minutes.

Lastly, add the drained cooked pasta, parmesan, and basil. Toss to combine. Add a portion of the reserved pasta water to thin the sauce if necessary. Serve hot.

INGREDIENTS

Butternut Squash – 1½ pounds, peeled, ½-inch diced

Olive Oil – 5 tablespoons, divided

Garlic – 8 cloves, minced

Yellow Onion – 1 large, ¼-inch diced

Red Onion – 1 large, ¼-inch diced

Red Bell Pepper – 1 large, ¼-inch diced

Crushed Tomatoes – 1 (15-ounce) can, San Marzano

Butter – 2 tablespoons, unsalted

Kosher Salt – 2 teaspoons, divided

Black Pepper – 2 teaspoons, divided

Sugar – 2 teaspoons, granulated

Capers – 2 tablespoons, drained

Basil – ½ cup, freshly chopped

Heavy Cream – ¼ cup

Parmesan Cheese – ½ cup, freshly grated

Rigatoni – 3 cups, dry pasta, cooked al dente

Pasta Water – ¼ cup, reserved

PREPARATION NOTES

Yield – Serves 6

A LITTLE STORY

One cool autumn evening I won our little contest for who got to cook dinner. With no real plan I invented this as I went along using my "a little of this, and a little of that" method. This immediately became one of Ryan's most favorite dishes I have created. He repeatedly reminded me to write it down. I forgot. Two years later (after a stare-down with Ryan) I finally committed to re-creating the dish. I was being judged on replicating the exact taste, texture, and flavor. Happily I succeeded. When testing recipes, even if you are unsure of the outcome, write it down as you go! Masterpieces sometimes happen when you are not even trying!

NOTES

_____

_____

_____

_____

_____

_____

_____

_____

Sole Meunière

A CLASSIC FRENCH DISH THAT IS ALWAYS IN STYLE

DIRECTIONS

Preheat the oven to 250 degrees F. Line a baking sheet with parchment paper and set aside.

Place the sole filets between layers of paper towels and thoroughly pat dry.

Next, combine the flour, panko bread crumbs, salt, and pepper in a shallow dish or plate.

Thoroughly coat each side of the sole filets in the flour mixture and set aside.

In a large sauté pan heat 3 tablespoons of butter over medium heat until the butter is melted and lightly browned. Place 2 sole filets in the pan and cook for 2 to 3 minutes. Turn carefully with a thin spatula and continue to cook for 2 to 3 minutes on the other side. Place the filets on the baking sheet and transfer to oven to keep warm. Repeat the same process until all the filets are cooked.

In the same sauté pan pour the lemon juice and add 3 tablespoons of butter. Bring to a simmer.

To serve, plate the filets and spoon the lemon butter sauce over the filets. Sprinkle with parsley, salt, and pepper. Serve immediately.

INGREDIENTS

Flour – 1 cup

Panko Bread Crumbs – ½ cup

Kosher Salt – 3 teaspoons

Black Pepper – 3 teaspoons

Sole (fresh) – 12 filets, about 4 ounces each

Butter – 15 tablespoons, unsalted, divided

Lemon Juice – 3 tablespoons

Flat Leaf Parsley – 2 tablespoons, freshly chopped

PREPARATION NOTES

Yield – Serves 6

REMEMBER THIS

When buying your sole filets ask your fish monger to check for any tiny bones that may have been left behind. If fresh sole is not available you can use walleye or even tilapia instead!

NOTES

Stilton & Pear Macaroni

SOPHISTICATED MAC N' CHEESE THAT IS JUST AS COMFORTING

DIRECTIONS

Preheat oven to 400 degrees F.

Butter a large shallow baking dish with 1 tablespoon of butter. Set aside.

Next, in a 12-inch sauté pan, heat 1 tablespoon of butter over medium heat.

Add onions, shallots, pears, 1 teaspoon of salt, and 1 teaspoon of pepper and sauté for 6 to 8 minutes, stirring occasionally, until just translucent.

Add garlic and continue cooking for an additional 2 minutes. Remove from heat and transfer into a large bowl. Set aside.

In a small sauce pan over medium heat, gently heat the milk to just below the simmering point. Remove from heat and set aside.

Next, in a medium sauce pan, over medium heat, melt 4 tablespoons of butter. Stir in the flour and cook for 2 minutes, stirring constantly.

Next, pour in the heated milk, 1 teaspoon of salt, 1 teaspoon of pepper, and allspice. Continue cooking for 5 to 6 minutes, whisking constantly until it thickens.

Remove from the heat and whisk in both cheeses. Then, add the cheese mixture into the onion mixture and add cooked pasta. Toss to coat.

Transfer mixture into the prepared pan.

In a small bowl, combine the bread crumbs and olive oil and mix well. Sprinkle the pasta with the bread crumb mixture. Dot the top with pea-sized bits of cold butter.

Bake until golden brown and bubbly, about 10 to 12 minutes. Remove from the oven and let stand 5 minutes before serving.

REMEMBER THIS!

You can also make this in advance and store in the refrigerator overnight. Simply allow to first rest at room temperature for about 20 minutes and then bake for 12 to 15, or until bubbly!

INGREDIENTS

Yellow Onion – 1 large, ¼-inch diced

Garlic – 4 cloves, minced

Shallot – 1 large, minced

Bosc Pears – 3, peeled, cored and ¼-inch diced

Flour – 6 tablespoons, divided

Butter – 6 tablespoons, unsalted, divided

Half-n-Half – 3 cups

Olive Oil – 1 tablespoon

Kosher Salt – 2 teaspoons, divided

Black Pepper – 2 teaspoons, divided

Allspice – ½ teaspoon

Gruyere Cheese – 1½ cups, grated

Stilton Blue Cheese – ¾ pound, crumbled

Dried Bread Crumbs – 1 cup, plain

Medium Pasta Shells – 1½ pounds, cooked al dente

PREPARATION NOTES

Bake – 10 to 12 minutes

Yield – Serves 6 to 8 people

NOTES

_____

_____

_____

_____

_____

_____

_____

_____

_____

Vegetable Pot Pie
HOME-STYLE COMFORT FOOD AT ITS BEST

DIRECTIONS

Crust

In the bowl of a food processor, fitted with a steel blade, add the flour, butter, sugar, white pepper, and ½ teaspoon of salt. Pulse the food processor 10 times or until the butter is the size of small peas.

Next, with the food processor running, slowly add the cold water down the feed tube. Add just enough for the dough to come together into single mass. Turn the mixture out onto a floured surface and quickly shape into a ball. Cover the dough ball in plastic wrap and refrigerate for 30 minutes.

White Sauce

In a small sauce pan bring the milk to a simmer. Remove from the heat and set aside

In a large sauce pan melt 8 tablespoons (1 stick) of butter over low heat. Add the flour and continue to cook for another 1 to 2 minutes, stirring constantly with a wooden spoon.

Pour the hot milk over the butter mixture. Add the salt and black pepper and continue cooking for another 5 to 6 minutes, stirring constantly using a whisk.

Vegetable Filling

In a large sauté pan heat the olive oil over medium heat. Add potatoes, carrots, and both onions. Cook for 8 to 10 minutes, or until the vegetables are tender.

Add the shallots, garlic, thyme, and string beans. Sauté for another 5 minutes.

Transfer all the vegetables into a large bowl and add the peas, corn, gruyere, and the white sauce. Stir together until well combined.

Preheat the oven to 400 degrees F. Butter a 9 x 13 x 2-inch baking dish.

Pour the entire vegetable mixture into the prepared pan.

Remove the dough from the refrigerator and roll it out to be just slightly larger than the baking dish. Place the dough over the baking dish and tuck under the edges of the dough. Place 3 large slits in the middle of the dough to allow steam to escape. Sprinkle with more salt, black pepper, and a light dusting of sugar.

Bake for 40 to 45 minutes, or until the crust is golden brown.

Allow to rest for 10 minutes before serving.

INGREDIENTS

Vegetable Filling

Shallot – 1 large, finely chopped

Garlic – 8 cloves, chopped

Yellow Onion – 1 large, ¼-inch diced

French String Beans – 1 cup, ½-inch length

Yukon Gold Potato – 1 large, peeled, ½-inch diced

Sweet Potato – 1 large, peeled, ½-inch diced

Carrots – 2 large, peeled, ½-inch diced

Red Onion – 1 medium, ¼-inch diced

Frozen Peas – 1½ cups

Frozen Corn – 1½ cups

Olive Oil – 4 tablespoons

Thyme – 2 teaspoons, freshly minced

Gruyere – 1 cup

White Sauce

Butter – 1 stick, unsalted

Flour – ½ cup

Milk – 4 cups

Kosher Salt – 1 tablespoon

Black Pepper – 1 tablespoon

Crust

Flour – 1½ cups

Butter – 1 stick, unsalted, very cold

Water – 8 tablespoons, iced

White Pepper – ½ teaspoon

Kosher Salt – ½ teaspoon

Sugar – 2 teaspoons, granulated

PREPARATION NOTES

Bake – 40 to 45 minutes

Yield – Serves 6

Desserts
DELIGHTFUL IDEAS FOR A SWEET FINALE THAT WILL BE REMEMBERED

Brown Butter Cake

THE NEW CLASSIC YELLOW CAKE

DIRECTIONS

In a small sauté pan, heat the 3 sticks of butter over low-medium heat for 10 to 12 minutes stirring occasionally. The butter will develop a subtly nutty aroma.

Scrape the butter and browned bits into a heat-proof bowl and transfer to the refrigerator for 1 hour.

Preheat oven to 325 degrees F. Butter and flour two 9-inch cake pans.

In a medium bowl sift together the flour, salt, and baking powder.

Remove the butter from the refrigerator and transfer into the bowl of an electric mixer fitted with a paddle attachment. Add the sugar and mix until light and fluffy, about 3 to 5 minutes.

Next, reduce the mixer speed to low and add the vanilla, egg yolks, and then the whole eggs.

Next, add the flour and milk alternately to mixture, beginning and ending with the flour. Mix until just combined.

Divide the batter evenly between the prepared pans. Bake for 35 to 40 minutes, until golden brown or the end of a cake tester, when inserted into the middle, comes out clean.

Remove the cakes from the oven and let cool in the pans for 20 minutes, then remove from the pans to cool completely.

INGREDIENTS

Butter – 3 sticks, unsalted

Flour – 2¼ cups, all-purpose

Kosher Salt – 1 teaspoon

Sugar – 1¾ cups, granulated

Baking Powder – 2¼ teaspoons

Vanilla – 2 teaspoons, pure extract

Eggs – 3 extra-large yolks, plus 2 extra-large whole

Milk – 1 ⅓ cups

PREPARATION NOTES

Bake – 35 to 40 minutes

Yield – 9-inch layer cake

A LITTLE STORY

This recipe is very special to Ryan and me. It was one of the three cake flavors I baked for one of the tiers of our wedding cake. It is wonderfully moist and the nutty flavor of the butter makes this cake a recipe that people are sure to never forget.

NOTES

_____

_____

_____

_____

_____

_____

_____

_____

By the Pound Cake

SO SIMPLE YET SO INCREDIBLY DELICIOUS AND VERSATILE

DIRECTIONS

Preheat oven to 350 degrees F.

Lightly butter and flour 2 loaf pans.

In the bowl of an electric mixer fitted with a paddle attachment, cream together the butter and sugar on medium speed until light and fluffy.

With the mixer turned to low speed, add vanilla, lemon zest, honey, and the eggs one at a time, allowing each to fully incorporate. Turn the mixer off.

Next, in a large bowl sift together the flour, salt, baking powder, and baking soda.

With the mixer running on low speed, add the flour and buttermilk alternately, beginning and ending with the flour.

Scrape down the sides and bottom of the mixing bowl and transfer the batter evenly between the prepared pans. Tap the pans on a flat surface to release as many air bubbles as possible.

Transfer pans into the oven and bake for 50 to 60 minutes, or until a toothpick inserted in the middle of the loaf comes out clean.

Once you have removed the loaves from the oven, allow them to cool in the pans for 10 minutes. Then, turn them out onto a wire rack to cool completely. Slice and serve hot, or at room temperature.

INGREDIENTS

Butter – 2 sticks, unsalted, room temperature

Eggs – 4 extra-large, room temperature

Flour – 3 cups, all-purpose

Baking Powder – ½ teaspoon

Baking Soda – ½ teaspoon

Kosher Salt – ¾ teaspoon

Buttermilk – 1 cup, room temperature

Vanilla – 1½ teaspoons, pure extract

Honey – ¼ cup

Lemon Zest – 1 tablespoon, fresh zest

Sugar – 2 cups, granulated

PREPARATION NOTES

Yield – 2 loaves

A TASTY IDEA

This versatile pound cake can be served for dessert with a dollop of whipped cream, made as the base for the Pound Cake Trifle (page 187), or even part of a breakfast parfait with fresh fruit and yogurt. These loaves freeze fabulously. Simply wrap them individually in plastic wrap and seal in a large freezer bag. Remove from the freezer three hours before you want to serve.

NOTES

_____

_____

_____

_____

_____

_____

_____

_____

Caramel Cake with Salted Caramel Buttercream

SALTY, SWEET, AND OH-SO-RICH

DIRECTIONS

Cake

Preheat oven to 350 degrees F. Butter and flour two 8-inch round cake pans and line the bottoms with parchment paper.

In a large bowl sift together the flour, baking powder, and salt. Set aside.

In the bowl of an electric mixer, fitted with a paddle attachment, cream together the butter and sugar on medium speed for 5 minutes, until light and fluffy. With the mixer running, add the eggs, one at a time, allowing each to be fully incorporated, then add the vanilla and sour cream and combine well.

Next, add flour and buttermilk alternately to the mixture, beginning and ending with flour. Mix until just incorporated.

Divide the batter evenly between the prepared pans. Bake for 25 to 30 minutes, until golden brown or when the end of a cake tester, inserted into the middle, comes out clean.

Remove the cakes from the oven and allow to cool completely (in the pans) on a wire rack.

Buttercream

For the buttercream, start by pouring the sugar and water into a small sauce pan over medium-high heat. Bring to a boil, and cook until it turns deep amber in color, swirling the pan NOT stirring.

Remove the pan from the heat and slowly add the heavy cream and vanilla. The mixture will bubble up wildly, so do this step very carefully. Whisk until smooth. Allow the caramel to cool, about 30 minutes.

In the bowl of an electric mixer, fitted with a paddle attachment, mix the butter and salt on medium speed until light and fluffy. Reduce the speed to low, and slowly add the powdered sugar, mixing until thoroughly combined.

Increase the speed to high and slowly pour the cooled caramel into the mixture. Mix until light and fluffy, about 2 to 3 minutes.

To frost the cake, transfer one cake to a cake stand or large platter. Using an offset spatula evenly spread the top of the cake with a layer of frosting. Place the second cake on top of the first. Spread the remaining frosting over the top and sides of both layers. Garnish with fresh raspberries and serve.

INGREDIENTS

Cake

Flour – 3 cups, all-purpose

Light Brown Sugar – 2¼ cups, lightly packed

Butter – 2 sticks, unsalted, room temperature

Eggs – 4 extra-large, room temperature

Buttermilk – 1¼ cups, room temperature

Sour Cream – ¼ cup

Vanilla – 2½ teaspoons

Baking Powder – 2 teaspoons

Kosher Salt – ¼ teaspoon

Buttercream

Sugar – ½ cup, granulated

Heavy Cream – ½ cup

Water – ¼ cup

Vanilla – 2½ teaspoons

Butter – 1 pound, unsalted, room temperature

Kosher Salt – 1 teaspoon

Powdered Sugar – 3 cups, sifted

PREPARATION NOTES

Bake – 25 to 30 minutes

Yield – 8-inch layer cake

NOTES

_____

_____

_____

_____

_____

_____

_____

_____

Crazy Gooey Brownies

BE SURE TO HAVE A GALLON OF MILK ON HAND FOR THIS DECADENT TREAT

DIRECTIONS

Preheat oven to 350 degrees F. Lightly butter and flour a 9 x 13-inch baking pan.

In a heat-proof bowl, over barely simmering water, melt the butter, sugar, and chopped chocolate (milk and dark), stirring occasionally until the chocolate is just melted, about 10 minutes (be patient, burnt chocolate is not yummy). Then, let the mixture cool to room temperature.

Next, sift the flour, cocoa powder, salt, and baking powder into a medium-sized bowl and set aside.

In the bowl of an electric mixer, fitted with a paddle attachment and set to medium speed, beat the chocolate mixture until it is shiny.

With the mixer still running, add the eggs one at a time allowing each to fully incorporate. Then, add the vanilla.

Next, set the mixer to low speed and slowly add the dry ingredients until just moistened.

Pour the batter into the prepared pan and smooth out the top with the back of the spatula.

Place the pan into the oven and bake until the edges are crisp and the top is set, about 25 to 27 minutes. (Because the center of the brownies will be slightly soft, a toothpick inserted will not come out clean—this is alright).

Remove the pan from the oven and allow to cool completely.

Cut the brownies into 3 x 3-inch squares. Pour a glass of milk, and indulge!

A LITTLE TIP

Once completely cooled in the pan, transfer to the refrigerator for 20 minutes and then cut into squares. Not only is this an easy way to cut brownies, but you get a perfect square every time! Just remember to allow the brownies to come to room temperature before you serve them!

INGREDIENTS

Milk Chocolate – 8 ounces, chopped

Dark Chocolate – 8 ounces, chopped

Cocoa Powder – ½ cup, unsweetened

Butter – 1½ sticks, unsalted, room temperature

Sugar – 1 cup, granulated

Flour – 1 cup, all-purpose

Baking Powder – 2 teaspoons

Kosher Salt – ¼ teaspoon

Eggs – 4 extra-large

Vanilla – 1½ tablespoons, pure extract

PREPARATION NOTES

Bake – 25 to 27 minutes

Yield – 12 brownies

NOTES

Edible Candied Flowers

AN UNFORGETTABLE GARNISH THAT IS BRIGHT AND COLORFUL

DIRECTIONS

Holding each flower by the stem, use a small paintbrush to apply a thin layer of the egg white, coating each side of the petals.

Dust the painted flower with super fine sugar, being sure to coat both sides of the petals. Gently shake off any excess sugar. Set aside to dry on a wire rack or parchment-lined sheet tray.

INGREDIENTS

Egg Whites – 2 extra-large, lightly beaten

Super Fine Sugar – ½ cup

Edible Flowers – 15 to 20

PREPARATION NOTES

Yield – 15 to 20 flowers

A LITTLE TIP

Edible flowers can be found in specialty food stores, typically where fresh herbs are kept. You can also ask your local florist or garden center for a list of edible flower species.

HERE'S AN IDEA

Use these to decorate cakes, cupcakes, or even on top of a salad! Edible Candied Flowers are also perfect for a tea party-themed birthday celebration (for little girls and ladies alike)!

NOTES

_____

_____

_____

_____

_____

_____

_____

_____

French Apple Tart

AN AMERICAN TAKE ON A FRENCH CLASSIC

DIRECTIONS

Dough

In the bowl of a food processor fitted with a steel blade, add the flour, butter, salt, and 2 tablespoons of sugar. Pulse 10 times or until the butter is the size of small peas. With the motor running slowly add the cold water down the feed tube, adding just enough until the dough comes together and forms a ball. Turn the mixture out onto a floured surface and quickly shape into a ball. Cover in plastic wrap and refrigerate for 1 hour.

Preheat oven to 400 degrees F. Line a sheet pan with parchment paper.

On a lightly floured surface, roll out the dough to roughly 11 x 15-inches. Trim the edges evenly using a small knife. Place the dough onto the sheet pan and set aside.

Fruit

Peel and core the apples. Slice the apples into ¼-inch thick slices and arrange them on the prepared dough in straight rows, slightly overlapping each slice. Repeat this process until the entire surface of the dough is covered.

Next, brush the tops of the apples with 2 tablespoons of room temperature butter and sprinkle with 4 tablespoons of sugar.

Bake the tart for 50 minutes to 1 hour, or until the edges are nicely browned. Once done, remove the tart from the oven and brush with honey-apple butter. Sprinkle with 3 tablespoons of brown sugar and using a kitchen torch, brûlée the sugar until it caramelizes evenly. Allow to cool and serve either warm or at room temperature.

INGREDIENTS

Flour – 2 cups, all-purpose

Kosher Salt – ½ teaspoon

Sugar – 6 tablespoons, granulated, divided

Butter (cold) – 1½ sticks, unsalted, diced

Butter – 2 tablespoons, unsalted, room temperature

Water – ½ cup ice water

Apples (Pink Lady) – 4

Honey-Apple Butter – ½ cup

Brown Sugar – 3 tablespoons, for garnish

PREPARATION NOTES

Bake – 50 to 60 minutes

Yield – Serves 6

HERE'S AN IDEA

Instead of using 1 variety of apple, mix it up with three, or even four (but avoid sour or tart apples). Use differently colored apples and create a unique pattern of your own.

NOTES

_____

_____

_____

_____

_____

_____

_____

_____

Honey Lavender Truffles

A SUBTLE BLEND OF FLAVORS, SOPHISTICATED TASTE, YET EASY TO MAKE

DIRECTIONS

In a small sauce pan combine the heavy cream and lavender. Heat to just below the boiling point, and then remove from heat. Cover and let steep for 5 minutes.

Strain the cream into another small sauce pan, pressing down on the lavender making sure to extract as much liquid as possible. Add the honey and salt and bring to a boil.

Remove from the heat and add 2 cups of the chopped chocolate. Stir until smooth.

Pour the finished ganache into a small bowl, cover tightly with plastic wrap and refrigerate for 1 hour.

Remove the ganache from the refrigerator and allow to sit at room temperature for 10 minutes.

Using a 1-inch scoop or teaspoon, scoop out balls of ganache and place onto a sheet pan lined with parchment paper. After you have scooped all the ganache, roll each one by hand into a ball.

Place the cocoa powder into a shallow bowl and roll each truffle through it to coat. Once finished, repeat for a second coat.

Next, in a glass heat-proof bowl over simmering water, melt the remaining 1 cup of chocolate, stirring constantly.

Drizzle each truffle with the melted chocolate and garnish with 3 to 4 dried lavender pieces.

Let set completely, at room temperature, before serving (about 1 hour).

REMEMBER THIS

Actual truffles found in the wild are not perfect and each one is uniquely shaped. Similarly, each of your chocolate truffles should be unique—that is the charm of truffles!

INGREDIENTS

Heavy Cream – ½ cup

Dried Lavender – 3 tablespoons, plus more for garnish

Honey – 4 tablespoons

Milk Chocolate – 3 cups, chopped, divided

Cocoa Powder – ¼ cup, unsweetened

Kosher Salt – $\frac{1}{8}$ teaspoon

PREPARATION NOTES

Yield – Makes 24 pieces

NOTES

_____

_____

_____

_____

_____

_____

_____

_____

Meringues with Raspberry Curd

A LIGHT AND AIRY DESSERT WITH STUNNINGLY DELICIOUS FLAVOR

DIRECTIONS

Meringues

Preheat the oven to 200 degrees F. Line a baking sheet with parchment paper.

In the bowl of an electric mixer fitted with the whisk attachment, beat the egg whites, cream of tartar, lemon juice, lemon zest, and salt on medium speed until frothy. Increase the mixer speed to high and add the sugar. Beat until the whites form stiff peaks.

Fill a pastry bag fitted with a large round or star tip and pipe the meringue into a 4-inch circle. Then, pipe another layer of meringue onto the edge of the first layer to form the sides of the meringue shells.

Place in the oven and bake for 2 hours. Once the meringues have finished baking, turn off the oven and allow to rest in the oven for 4 to 6 hours. At this point the meringue shells can be stored in an air tight container for up to 7 days if you want to make the components in advance.

Raspberry Curd

Melt the butter in a large sauce pan over medium heat. Add the raspberries, egg yolks, sugar, and salt. Cook for 10 to 12 minutes, stirring frequently while mashing the berries.

Pour the mixture through a coarse sieve set over a medium-sized glass bowl. Press the mixture through the sieve with the back of a wooden spoon, trying to extract as much liquid as possible. Stir in the lemon juice. To store, press a piece of plastic wrap directly on the surface of the raspberry curd and refrigerate. The raspberry curd will stay fresh in the refrigerator for up to 7 days.

Grand Marnier® Whipped Cream

In the bowl of an electric mixer, fitted with a whisk attachment, whip the heavy cream on high speed until it starts to thicken. Add the sugar, vanilla, and Grand Mariner® and continue to beat until stiff peaks form.

To assemble, fill each meringue shell with raspberry curd and top with a big scoop of the whipped cream. Garnish with fresh raspberries and a sprinkle of lemon zest.

INGREDIENTS

Meringues

Eggs Whites – 3 extra-large

Sugar – ¾ cups, granulated

Cream of Tartar – $\frac{1}{8}$ teaspoon

Kosher Salt – $\frac{1}{8}$ teaspoon

Lemon Zest – 1 tablespoon

Lemon Juice – 1 teaspoon

Raspberry Curd

Butter – 1 stick, unsalted

Raspberries – 1 pint, plus more for garnish

Egg Yolks – 5 extra-large, lightly beaten

Sugar – ¾ cup, granulated

Kosher Salt – $\frac{1}{8}$ teaspoon

Lemon Juice – 2 teaspoons

Grand Mariner® Whipped Cream

Heavy Cream – 2 cups, very cold

Sugar – 3 tablespoons

Vanilla Extract – 2 teaspoon

Grand Mariner® – 1½ tablespoons

NOTES

_____

_____

_____

_____

_____

_____

_____

_____

A SIMPLE TRICK

Make the meringues and raspberry curd in advance. When it is time for dessert make the whipped cream and assemble! Meringues with Raspberry Curd are a chic and no-sweat dessert!

PREPARATION NOTES

Bake – 10 to 12 minutes (4 to 6 hours rest time)

Yield – Serves 6

Mouthwatering Molasses Cookies

CRUNCHY ON THE OUTSIDE AND GOOEY IN THE MIDDLE—EXACTLY RIGHT

DIRECTIONS

In a small sauce pan over low heat, melt the butter. Once melted, add 2 cups of sugar and the molasses, stirring frequently, until sugar is dissolved. Remove from heat and let cool.

In the bowl of an electric mixer fitted with a paddle attachment, beat the eggs and cooled molasses mixture on medium speed until well mixed.

In a large bowl, sift together the flour, salt, baking soda, cinnamon, ginger, and cloves. With the mixer set to medium speed, gradually add the flour mixture and beat until smooth. The dough will be very stiff.

Cover the dough tightly with plastic wrap and place in the refrigerator for 2 hours.

Pour ½ cup of sugar onto a small plate.

Preheat oven to 375 degrees F and line a half sheet pan with a piece of parchment paper.

Remove the dough from the refrigerator and form into 1½-inch balls by rolling the dough between the palms of your hands until very smooth and a bit shiny. Then roll half of each ball in the sugar and place 2½-inches apart on the sheet pan, sugared side up.

Bake for 16 to 17 minutes until the edges are browned and crisp.

Transfer to a wire rack to cool completely (if you can wait that long).

INGREDIENTS

Butter – 1½ sticks, unsalted

Sugar – 2½ cups, granulated, divided

Eggs – 2 extra-large

Molasses – ½ cup, dark

Baking Soda – 4 teaspoons

Flour – 4 cups, all-purpose

Cinnamon – 2¼ teaspoons

Ginger – 1¾ teaspoons

Cloves – ¾ teaspoon

Kosher Salt – 1 teaspoon

PREPARATION NOTES

Bake – 16 to 17 minutes

Yield – 20 cookies

A LITTLE STORY

Ryan's Oma made a version of these cookies since 1958! We have bumped up the ingredients to make them even more amazing (if that's possible). We hope this family-inspired recipe is one you and yours will enjoy for years to come!

NOTES

Pound Cake Trifle

THE PERFECT DESSERT AS FRESH BERRIES COME INTO SEASON

DIRECTIONS

In a large bowl, combine all the berries and toss with 1 tablespoon of sugar. Let stand for 10 minutes to macerate.

Next, cut the By the Pound Cake (page 171) loaf into ½-inch cubes.

In the bowl of an electric mixer fitted with the whisk attachment, pour in the heavy cream and whisk on high speed (gently increasing the speed to prevent splattering out of the bowl). When the heavy cream begins to thicken add the remaining sugar, vanilla, orange liqueur, and orange zest and continue to whip on high speed until it forms stiff peaks. Turn off the mixer and set aside.

Choose a clear glass trifle dish or a deep high-sided bowl to assemble your trifle.

Start by placing a layer of whipped cream on the bottom of your serving dish. Then add a layer of pound cake, followed by a layer of berries. Repeat this process until you have used up all the components. Be sure to end with the last of the berry mixture on the very top. Place a dollop of whipped cream in the center of the berries, sprinkle with a bit more orange zest, and serve.

The trifle can sit at room temperature for up to 3 hours.

INGREDIENTS

Strawberries – 1 pint, rinsed, hulled and sliced to ¼-inch pieces

Blueberries – 1 cup, rinsed

Raspberries – 1 cup, rinsed

Blackberries – 1 cup, rinsed

Sugar – 4 tablespoons, granulated, divided

Heavy Whipping Cream – 1 pint, very cold

Vanilla – 1 teaspoon

Orange Liqueur – 2 tablespoons, Grand Marnier® recommended

Orange Zest – 2 tablespoons, freshly zested

By the Pound Cake – 1 loaf (page 171)

PREPARATION NOTES

Yield – Serves 8

A FRESH IDEA

With its vibrant colors this could easily be your centerpiece on a food table. And, Pound Cake Trifle is best served at room temperature.

NOTES

Rich Chocolate Ganache Cup Cakes
THESE DECADENT LITTLE CAKES ARE SO CHOCOLATY AND MOIST

DIRECTIONS

Batter

Preheat the oven to 325 degrees F and line a muffin pan (large cups) with paper liners.

Next, cream the butter and sugar until light and fluffy using an electric mixer fitted with a paddle attachment. Add the eggs carefully—1 at a time—and combine thoroughly. Then, pour in the vanilla and the chocolate syrup and mix well.

For the best results sift together your flour and unsweetened cocoa powder. Then, gently add the dry mixture to your mixing bowl and mix until just combined (do not over-mix or your cupcakes will be unpleasantly dense).

Next, scoop the batter equally into the muffin cups and bake for 30 minutes, or until just set in the middle. Do not over-bake the cupcakes. Let them cool thoroughly in the muffin tin.

Ganache & Assembly

Heat the heavy cream and chocolate chips in a double boiler over simmering water until smooth and warm. Stir occasionally. In this step you are melting and heating the mixture, not cooking it as it will burn.

Finally, once the cupcakes have cooled, dip the tops of the cupcakes into the ganache and enjoy! The ganache will remain soft and creamy and will not set hard.

Do not refrigerate.

INGREDIENTS

Batter

Butter – ¼ pound, unsalted, room temperature

Sugar – 1 cup

Salt – ¼ teaspoon

Flour – 1 cup all-purpose flour

Eggs – 4 extra-large, room temperature

Vanilla – 1 tablespoon, pure extract

Cocoa Powder – ¼ cup, unsweetened powder

Chocolate Syrup – 16 ounces

Ganache

Heavy Cream – ½ cup

Chocolate Chips – 8 ounces, semisweet

PREPARATION NOTES

Bake – 30 minutes

Yield – 12 cupcakes

NOTES

_____

_____

_____

_____

_____

_____

_____

_____

Vanilla Bean Buttercream

THIS ULTRA-THICK AND RICH FROSTING TASTES LIKE MELTED VANILLA ICE CREAM

DIRECTIONS

Start by combining water and sugar in a small sauce pan and bring to a boil. Once boiling, cook until it reaches 235 degrees F, using a candy thermometer.

Separate the whites of 4 extra-large eggs. Discard the yolks.

In the bowl of an electric mixer, fitted with the whisk attachment, whip the egg whites until they form soft peaks, about 3 to 4 minutes.

Once the sugar syrup reaches 235 degrees F slowly and carefully pour down the inside of the mixing bowl with the mixer set to low speed.

Next, set the mixer to medium-high speed and continue whipping the mixture until light, fluffy, and almost completely cooled, or about 10 minutes.

With the mixer still running add the vanilla and vanilla bean.

Lastly, add the softened butter, 1 tablespoon at a time, until the frosting is thick and fluffy.

INGREDIENTS

Sugar – 2 cups

Egg Whites – 4 extra-large

Water – ¼ cup

Butter – 1¾ pounds, unsalted, room temperature

Vanilla – 1 tablespoon, pure extract

Vanilla Bean – 1 large bean, seeded

A TASTY IDEA

This is not your mother's lumpy icing we all had when we were little. Thick and truly luxurious, this buttercream is perfect for a simple sheet cake or a towering tiered masterpiece!

NOTES

_____

_____

_____

_____

_____

_____

_____

_____

_____

Velvety Hot Chocolate

THE PERFECT MORNING TREAT OR EVENING DELIGHT

DIRECTIONS

Start by heating the milk and half-and-half in a medium sauce pan over medium heat until it just begins to simmer.

Remove the pan from the heat and add all of the chocolate, cocoa power, vanilla, cinnamon, light brown sugar, salt, and caramel.

In the pan, whisk quickly until the mixture is smooth and the chocolate is completely melted.

Gently reheat on low heat, and then carefully pour into a very large measuring cup or pitcher. Use the pitcher to cleanly pour into cups and serve hot.

Garnish each cup with a marshmallow (or 2)!

INGREDIENTS

Milk Chocolate – 8 ounces, chopped

Dark Chocolate – 8 ounces, chopped

Cocoa Powder – ¼ cup, unsweetened

Half-and-Half – 2 cups

Whole Milk – 3 cups

Vanilla – 1½ teaspoons, pure extract

Cinnamon – ¼ teaspoon

Light Brown Sugar – 2 tablespoons

Kosher Salt – ⅛ teaspoon

Caramel Sauce – 4 tablespoons, good store-bought caramel

Marshmallows – 12 large pieces

PREPARATION NOTES

Yield – 6 servings

A LITTLE STORY

When Ryan and I were celebrating our first Christmas together I wanted to make something very special to sip while we sat under our Christmas tree and opened our presents. Regular hot chocolate would not do. After combining our favorite flavors of chocolate and caramel, Velvety Hot Chocolate was created! Now, we have a delicious tradition to look forward to every year (and any time we need rich pick-me-up)!

NOTES

Cheers!

COCKTAILS PERFECTED FOR ANY TOAST

Champagne Kiss

PERFECTED FOR UNFORGETTABLE ENTERTAINING

DIRECTIONS

Pour the cocoa powder onto a small plate. On another small plate pour just enough water to coat the bottom of the plate. Place the rim of a champagne flute into the water then directly into the cocoa powder to cover each rim.

Do this with all the champagne flutes.

Place a piece of chocolate in the bottom of each champagne flute and fill with champagne. Top with a slice of strawberry.

Here's to you!

INGREDIENTS

Champagne (your favorite) – 1 bottle

Dark Chocolate – 6 pieces, ½-inch

Strawberries – 6, ½-inch sliced

Cocoa Powder – ¼ cup

PREPARATION NOTES

Yield – Serves 6

A TASTY IDEA

Serve this elegant take on champagne during cocktail hour with our Craquelins Savoureux (page 53) for an unforgettable and decadent experience!

NOTES

Chilled Tequila

A REFINED SHOT OF TEQUILA TO BE SAVORED

DIRECTIONS

Pour the cinnamon onto a small plate. On another small plate pour just enough water to coat the bottom of the plate.

Place part of the rim of a cordial glass into the water and then directly into the cinnamon to coat the wet portion of the rim. Do this for the other five cordial glasses.

Fill a shaker with ice and add the tequila. Shake vigorously until well chilled.

Fill each glass evenly with tequila.

INGREDIENTS

Tequila – 2 cups

Orange Wedges – For garnish

Cinnamon – ¼ cup

PREPARATION NOTES

Yield – Serves 6

A TASTY IDEA

For this aperitif I love the idea of using a cordial glass instead of a traditional shot glass for a more refined presentation. If you do not have cordial glasses in your bar cabinet try heading down to your local antique store, or even garage sales. Collecting and having a mixed-and-matched set of barware is a charming flare that makes each experience a little unique!

NOTES

Classic Vodka Martini

KNOWN THE WORLD OVER AS THE ULTIMATE MARTINI

DIRECTIONS

Fill each martini glass with ice and cold water and let sit for 5 minutes.

Pour the dry vermouth into a shaker filled with ice. Shake briskly and then pour out. Next, using the same ice, pour the vodka into the shaker and shake vigorously until well chilled.

Pour out the water and ice from each martini glass. Evenly pour the shaken vodka into each glass.

Garnish with 3 olives. Allow your guests to add a splash of fresh olive juice to taste for a dirty version.

INGREDIENTS

Vodka – 2 cups

Dry Vermouth – 1 ounce

Olive Juice – To taste

Blue Cheese Stuffed Olives – 18

PREPARATION NOTES

Yield – Serves 6

ALWAYS IN STYLE

From Fleming's Bond, to Jack Kennedy, to any evening involving a tuxedo, or just to enjoy, this classic will always be in style.

NOTES

_____

_____

_____

_____

_____

_____

_____

_____

CHEERS!

ℛM

Front Porch Lemonade

A REFRESHING ADULT-ONLY VERSION OF LEMONADE

DIRECTIONS

Start by hulling ½ pound of strawberries. Place the berries into the bowl of a food processor and pulse until smooth.

Pour the sugar onto a small plate. On another small plate pour just enough water to coat the bottom of the plate. Dip the rim of a double old fashioned glass into the water and then dip directly into the sugar to coat each rim. Do this for the other five glasses.

Next, fill the 6 sugar-rimmed double old fashioned glasses with ice. Pour the vodka, lemonade, pink lemonade powder, and strawberry purée into a pitcher and stir until well mixed and the powder has dissolved. Pour evenly into the glasses. Garnish with a slice of fresh lemon and serve.

INGREDIENTS

Lemonade – 3 cups

Vodka – 2 cups

Pink Lemonade Powder – 6 tablespoons

Fresh Strawberry Purée – $\frac{1}{3}$ cup

Sliced Lemon – For garnish

Sugar – ¼ cup, granulated, for garnish

PREPARATION NOTES

Yield – Serves 6

TRY THIS

Make this entire cocktail ahead of the party and keep it in the refrigerator in a pitcher and ready to be poured. Front Porch Lemonade also makes a fabulous beach or picnic drink. Simply pour into glass jars with lids and place into your cooler filled with ice. You will have an instant party, anywhere you go!

NOTES

_____

_____

_____

_____

_____

_____

_____

_____

_____

Mocha Martini

SERVED BEFORE DINNER, OR AFTER, IT IS ALWAYS A HIT

DIRECTIONS

In a pitcher combine the vodka, coffee and chocolate liqueurs, and heavy cream. Stir together until combined.

Decorate the inside of 6 martini glasses with a drizzle of chocolate syrup.

Fill a cocktail shaker with ice and half of the vodka mixture. Shake vigorously until well chilled. Pour evenly into 3 martini glasses. Repeat the process for the remaining 3 glasses.

Once all the martini glasses are filled garnish with a generous sprinkle of chocolate shavings and enjoy!

INGREDIENTS

Vodka – 3 cups

Coffee Liqueur – 1½ cups

Chocolate Liqueur – 1½ cups

Dark Chocolate Syrup – ⅓ cup, plus more for garnish

Heavy Cream – 3 tablespoons

Dark Chocolate Shavings – For garnish

PREPARATION NOTES

Yield – Serves 6

HERE'S AN IDEA

This cocktail turns to pure dessert when served with biscotti for dipping, or even a scoop of ice cream!

NOTES

_____

_____

_____

_____

_____

_____

_____

_____

Peach Cooler

REFRESHING AND LIGHT, IT IS PERFECT FOR SIPPING

DIRECTIONS

Fill 6 highball glasses with ice.

Combine the vodka and honey in a shaker filled with ice. Shake vigorously until the honey is incorporated into the vodka.

Fill each glass evenly with the shaken vodka and honey. Top off with peach nectar. Garnish with a fresh sprig of rosemary and a slice of ripened peach.

INGREDIENTS

Vodka – 2 cups

Peach Nectar – 2 cups, chilled

Honey – 2 tablespoons

Rosemary Sprig – For garnish

Peach Wedges – For garnish

PREPARATION NOTES

Yield – Serves 6

HERE'S AN IDEA

If you are having a party and want to serve this as your signature drink, make large amounts of the vodka and honey mixture ahead of time to avoid being stuck in the kitchen with a shaker all night! Pour the vodka into a carafe and keep it in a large ice bucket along with a carafe of peach nectar. Have the glasses, rosemary, and peach wedges on a side bar available to your guests.

A LITTLE TIP

Peach nectar can be found in the international isle of your grocery store, and often in the spirits section with other mixers.

NOTES

_____

_____

_____

_____

_____

_____

_____

_____

Pear & Thyme Cocktail

A SWEET, SOUR, AND SAVORY COCKTAIL THAT IS PERFECT FOR ALL YOUR TASTE BUDS

DIRECTIONS

Begin by filling 6 double old fashioned glasses with ice.

Pour the gin, lime juice, and thyme leaves into a cocktail shaker filled with ice. Shake vigorously until chilled.

Pour evenly into each glass and top off with pear nectar. Garnish each drink with a fresh thyme sprig and a floating slice of lime.

INGREDIENTS

Tanqueray Rangpur® Gin – 2 cups

Pear Nectar – 3 cups, chilled

Lime Juice – 2 tablespoons, freshly squeezed

Thyme Leaves – 2 tablespoons, fresh

Lime Slices – For garnish

Thyme Sprigs – For garnish

PREPARATION NOTES

Yield – Serves 6

A TASTY IDEA

This cocktail pairs (no pun-intended) well with the Sautéed Onion & Cream Cheese Dip (page 71) for the happiest of hours-cocktail hour!

HERE'S A TIP

Pear nectar can be found in the international isle of your grocery store, and often in the spirits section with other mixers.

NOTES

_____

_____

_____

_____

_____

_____

_____

_____

_____

The Lady

AN ELEGANT GLASS OF BUBBLY WITH A TWIST

DIRECTIONS

Load a stylish (but functional) shaker half-way with fresh ice, add the gin, lemon juice, and simple syrup and shake vigorously for 15 seconds.

Separately, pour the champagne into a fabulous stemmed flute, then strain the shaken gin mixture directly into the champagne.

Stir gently to preserve the champagne's bubbles, and toast!

INGREDIENTS

Gin – 2 parts

Lemon Juice – ½ part, freshly squeezed

Simple Syrup – $^1/_3$ part

Champagne (your favorite) – $1^1/_3$ parts

PREPARATION NOTES

Yield – Multiply parts to desired volume

GIVE IT A TRY

Elegantly simple, this drink gives you just the right balance of fresh citrus with a tingly potency.

SIMPLE SYRUP

Simple syrup is exactly that. Make this ahead of time and have on hand:

Pour 1 cup of water and 1 cup of sugar into a small sauce pan set over medium heat.

Allow to come to a boil and reduce by half.

Cool completely and transfer to a container of your choice.

NOTES

_____

_____

_____

_____

_____

_____

_____

The Ricky

AN ITALIAN CLASSIC WITH A TWIST—MORE LIKE A SPLASH

DIRECTIONS

Fill 6 double old fashioned glasses with ice. Pour ½ cup of amaretto into each glass.

Splash with 1 tablespoon of Grand Marnier®.

Sprinkle with ½ teaspoon of orange zest and garnish the rim with a fresh orange wedge.

INGREDIENTS

Amaretto – 3 cups, divided

Grand Marnier® – 6 tablespoons, divided

Orange Zest – For garnish

Orange Wedge – For garnish

PREPARATION NOTES

Yield – Serves 6

A LITTLE STORY

I created the Ricky in honor of my late daddy, Richard. One of his favorite aperitifs was amaretto on the rocks. He was Italian after all! With the addition of a luxurious splash of Grand Marnier® this updated and fabulous cocktail is one of our favorite summertime drinks. During the autumn add a pinch of cinnamon to add a bit of warmth. Cheers to a simple cocktail in honor of the spirit of a simply wonderful man, Ricky!

NOTES

Love Is In the Details

EVERYDAY ENTERTAINING WITH STYLE

Though your cuisine may be the center of attention, every great performance deserves the proper stage. This section provides guidance and a few simple rules to remember when planning any event, from a casual brunch to a themed soirée. When you give a little love to the details your event will be polished and will truly impress your guests with a sense of your own style. Let the entertaining begin!

Entertaining is more than just putting food on the table and making sure guests' wine glasses are full. It encompasses all of our senses all at once, which is what makes it such a fun part of our lives! You can throw a great party morning, noon, or night. It can be themed or casual, celebrating a special event or "just because." The reasons we entertain and how we do it are limitless.

With all of that choice and possibility it can sometimes be overwhelming to plan an event. And often we just repeat what we thought worked before because it seemed easier. But where is the fun in that? Hosting a morning brunch, afternoon luncheon, evening dinner, or any special event does not have to take the time or cause the stress that we often think it does.

Being a great host will always involve a little time for planning and preparation, but great entertaining is actually more of a mindset than anything else. Any event you host should be an extension of your own style and personality. Stay true to yourself and the details will fall into place more easily! That attention to detail will give your guests (even old friends) the sense that you think they are special and worth that extra bit of effort.

Never mind that your guests need not know how easy a satisfying dish was to prepare or how quickly a colorful tablescape was set out. Take pride in what you do for your guests. It will shine through and will be appreciated by those with whom you share your home, hearth, and heart!

Whether you are throwing a surprise birthday celebration for a little one, an intimate themed dinner party, an anniversary, or you just want to share a grand time with close friends, you can easily elevate your event to a memorable one by attending to a few basic details.

It is here that I have detailed some of my best tips for great entertaining results, as well as time and stress-saving tricks. These will help you to put together a great event while having a good time before, during, and afterward!

ENTERTAINING TIPS & TRICKS

My single most important rule for entertaining, and life in general, is to recognize that love is in the details! Try to remember and appreciate the little things that make everyday living with style fabulous and worth the effort!

I have lost count of how many dinner parties I have thrown, and while the vast majority went off without a hitch, a few have fallen flat—like lifeless champagne! Those few duds had one thing in common—not being organized and properly prepared. Simply put, being well organized is the key to any successful soirée!

MENU & PLANNING

Plan a fabulous and delicious menu! Choose your dishes to compliment the occasion or theme of your event and balance between starters, side dishes, and the main course. Are you serving a filling main course? Then prepare fewer or lighter complimentary side dishes. Are you planning a decadent dessert? Then less is more when it comes to extras like hearty breads or heavy starters.

—◦—

Make your shopping list ahead of time. Organize your ingredients for each dish onto separate sheet trays. This will keep you organized and help you to move things around easily when counter space becomes scarce. Staying organized makes for a more enjoyable time in the kitchen, and will actually save you time in the process!

—◦—

Decide what serving dishes you are going to use before you even begin cooking. Use sticky notes to organize and help you remember which menu items are going to be placed in which serving dish. This is especially helpful for buffet-style food tables.

—◦—

Prepare dishes ahead of time. Many dishes and ingredients will keep fresh in the refrigerator for a couple of days so take advantage of that little bit of down-time you may have while cooking dinner during other nights of the week. Organize your creations in one section of your refrigerator. Heat your dishes in the oven (never the microwave) and add fresh garnishes right before serving. Your guests will think you were toiling away in the kitchen all day.

—◦—

You do not have to make absolutely everything from scratch! There is no need to make your own crackers to serve with cheese, or to make your own croissants for breakfast, for example. Find brands that you love and trust—always taste them before you serve to your guests. Keep crackers well stocked in your pantry so you are ready to go at a moment's notice! After a quick trip to your local bakery put your baked goods on a parchment-lined sheet tray and warm them in a 200 degree F oven for a few minutes just before you are ready to start serving. Your house will smell like the bakery!

DINNERWARE & LINENS

White plates are simply the best for showcasing the dishes you have lovingly prepared for your guests. Remember, expensive does not always mean better. Choose a setting that is thin and has simple lines. No matter your entertaining style you will always have versatile dinnerware!

Pressing napkins and tablecloths is the last thing I want to do when I have four pans going on the stovetop and guests arriving in a matter of hours. Avoid unnecessary stress by pre-pressing your linens as soon as you have laundered them. Dedicate a special linen drawer or shelf where you have easy access to your linens. If ironing is a skill that has entirely passed you by, your local dry cleaner will do a wonderful job steaming away that mess of wrinkles.

TABLE, FLOWERS, & SERVICE

One of the easiest tricks to save yourself stress on the day of your party is to set your table the night before. You can take your time to make sure all of your details are in place, and you will have time to fix or work around any problems you might discover (like a torn tablecloth or wax-encrusted candle stick). This trick will leave you with more time on the day of your party for other details, or to just relax.

Buy flowers and arrange them one or two days in advance of your party. You can check off that quick task as well as allow the blooms to relax and open. Your arrangements will appear fuller and more natural. Remember to change the water daily in order to keep your flowers fresh and vibrant. For most cut stems you should use warm tap water. Your local florist is a great resource to help you choose beautiful fresh cut flowers that will last, and not be the most expensive thing on your table.

Antique silver trays are my signature entertaining trick! They are useful, beautiful, and inexpensive. I find them at garage sales, flea markets, and online. Buy many different sizes so you have the perfect one every time. It is amazing what they will do to elevate your party and add instant classic style!

Wine charms are not only a useful way for your guests to keep tabs on their glass, but are also a subtle and fun way to carry your theme throughout your soirée. Think of wine charms as jewelry for your stemware. Remember, they should be useful and should not interfere with the primary purpose of the glassware.

Wine coasters are an essential service item for your bar and table. Not only do they protect your table and other surfaces from the hard glass bottom of a wine bottle, but they also prevent drips that would otherwise leave you with a morning of stain removal for your linens. There are many variations of wine coasters, from modern to antique silver, to fit your style. They can also be used as service dishes for nuts, candies, and other nibbles served during cocktail hour.

ATMOSPHERE

Having a theme to your party and the food you serve is essential, but don't go overboard! Try not to be too literal with your tablescapes. Add smaller details that will evoke your theme's sentiment. By keeping it simple, it will always be chic and stylish!

Candles are a fantastic way to elevate the atmosphere of any party. Use unscented candles at your table or in the vicinity of your food table and entertaining space. An over-powering whiff of a sickly sweet or pungent candle will derail the wonderful aromas your guests should be raving about, those of your fabulous food and drink!

Music, music, music! It can make or break your party. Create playlists that will be appropriate to the time of day of your party, and to the theme of your food. Daytime events at breakfast, brunch, and lunch should be supported with cheery and happy music selections. A little French or Italian sidewalk café music can add some whimsy and frivolity while being easy on the ears. For dinner, I love to play Frank Sinatra and other great artists from his genre. Jazz it up with Horace Silver after dinner and while your guests are enjoying dessert, champagne, or an after dinner aperitif. Select music you would want to hear, and change it up through the night. Play varied artists within the same music genre.

Provide disposable hand towels for your guests in the bathroom. You can find these online or even at your local grocery store. They create a luxurious sensation and, with a few strategically placed candles, can transform any bathroom into a fabulous powder room.

SUNDRY ITEMS

When was the last time you received a paper invitation to dinner? If your soirée is planned with enough time in advance, try mailing (yes, with a stamp through the Post Office) a proper invitation! Your invitees will feel extra special with this little traditional detail. For those last-minute parties send an emailed version of an invitation.

When guests bring a host or hostess gift (which a courteous guest should do), be sure to steal away a moment with your guests to open the gift in front of them. Have a vase ready for any fresh cut flowers your guests may bring and space in your refrigerator for white wine or champagne. Always remember to send a thank you note for the gift.

With all of these simple tips and tricks in action I like to have a glass of champagne before the start of the party as a toast to a job well done and to relax a bit. Also, for the first hour or so I will be greeting and catching up with my guests as they arrive and it is hard to hug and shake hands with a glass in my hand!

BREAKFAST & BRUNCH

Breakfast and brunch are two of my favorite times to entertain and spend time with guests. The food is simple, comforting, easy to prepare and not fussy. Guests tend to be more casually relaxed. And brunch in particular is a perfect opportunity to pop a bottle of champagne before noon! Another added benefit to morning entertaining is having the rest of your day to relax (or shop!). Here are some of my tips for an effortless and elegant morning party:

Use placemats without a tablecloth for a more informal touch. Try using a fabric with a rustic feel and texture, like a woven natural fiber.

Be careful not to overcrowd the table with plates. Use one large dinner plate for each guest. The goal is to entertain simply and casually, leaving you with less to clean up afterward.

Serve your main course and side dishes on over-sized platters or even right from the pans off the stove. Breakfast is about waking up and taking in the day. The warm and steaming aromas of a freshly prepared meal arriving at the table will do the trick!

Arrange fresh and vibrant flowers in alternating sizes of juice glasses for an off-the-cuff touch. Flowers with a delicate scent or no scent at all work best for all tables.

Adding candles to your table in the morning creates an inviting and unexpected touch! Remember to always use unscented candles. You never want the smell of a candle to compete with aromas of your meal.

Choose a short-sided simple glass to serve water, juice, a short Bloody Mary, or even champagne at each place setting.

Use brightly colored napkins to add a pop of color and a little sunshine to your table.

Breakfast and brunch should be fun, upbeat, and cheery parties! Keeping it casual and earthy with little unexpected touches is the perfect way to ensure a fabulous and memorable time is had by all!

LUNCH & LUNCHEONS

When hosting an afternoon lunch I like to think back to when our grandmothers would have "the girls" over and how they always took so much pride in setting the table and preparing the food. No detail was left unnoticed! In today's world a leisurely lunch for most people (including myself) is a rare treat, so why not make it special! It is easy and here is how:

Use matching placemats and napkins for a coordinated look. I prefer to use plain linen—it is chic, not too busy, and easy to clean.

Choose a monochromatic color scheme. Soft colors instantly add elegance and allow your food and flowers to be the main events.

Flowers arranged in antique cordial glasses that surround clear hurricanes with white unscented candles will keep your table simple yet classically appointed.

A soup course is perfect for lunch, followed by a salad, and then a crostata. Each is easy to prepare and will create a sense of elegance as you move through a multi-course menu. Make sure your menu choices are filling, but not too heavy.

Use individual soup tureens and a large dinner plate for serving. All-white plates and dinnerware are my preference for a chic lunch.

Wooden chargers are the perfect way to add instant rustic style to your table. They are less formal than a silver or crystal option and still provide a finished element to your table.

I like to use a tall and simple wine glass. Whether your guests prefer red or white wine, you will be set!

Hosting a lunch can be oh-so-fabulous! Remember, a little glamour mixed in will go a long way. Lunch is often a forgotten opportunity for great entertaining. Take advantage of the bright daylight. Set an up-beat music playlist for your party and choose a bright and flavorful signature cocktail for a little extra pizzazz. These little details will create a confident and refined atmosphere that will leave your guests with a great impression and a good time had by all.

DINNER & SOIRÉES

When I begin planning a dinner party I very often create my event around a classic restaurant or bistro style. I keep the food delicious and inviting with a menu that showcases home-cooked dishes and I balance that by creating a table for my guests that will be remembered! I look to include elegant and classic touches for a très chic result that is actually easy to put together. Here is what works very well:

Use a tablecloth for a dinner with matching napkins. Classic crisp white cotton serves as a fabulous backdrop for silver, crystal, and most importantly the food!

Place cards are a fabulous must, even for groups of friends. Remember, this is an occasion and you want to create a special night for your guests!

Towering white unscented (and dripless) tapered candles are an easy way to create a dramatic look that will also add a bit of height to a table. I have many different types of candlesticks, but my favorites are a special pair of crystal that are regularly a part of my tablescapes.

When serving bread give each guest their own small butter knife. I like to place small dishes of room-temperature butter around the table. Each guest will have easy access and there will be less to have to pass around the table.

Chargers are an incredibly easy way to give your table that finishing touch. They add a bit of glamor and enhance the sense of the evening being a special event. Simple silver chargers add a bit of sparkle and reflection without competing with the other highlights of your table.

Flowers are an important part of an elegant dinner party tablescape. However, towering sculptures of flowers are for hotel lobbies. Flower arrangements should be short enough so that guests can see over them. Place a full bouquet of tulips in the center of the table as guests are mingling about. Just before your guests are seated replace the tulips with something shorter, like a single-stemmed hydrangea (my favorite flower)!

A footed glass or crystal bowl makes a perfect salad bowl for each guest. They add a little depth to your table. You can also use the same style of dish (for a different party, of course) for any dessert served in a bowl, such as a trifle.

Whether you are hosting an intimate Monday evening dinner with friends, or a Saturday night soirée with new faces, take a moment to consider how you want to make each and every time you sit at the table special. You have taken the time to extend an invitation and prepare fabulous food, so let your attention to detail carry over to your table top!

Recipe Index

RECIPE INDEX

ℜM

RECIPE INDEX

— ℛℳ —

Notes

Notes

IT IS ALWAYS BEST TO WRITE IT DOWN THE FIRST TIME

NOTES

ℛM

10069972R00134

Made in the USA
San Bernardino, CA
08 April 2014